THE GOLDEN AGE
OF
ONONDAGA LAKE RESORTS

Flying Airships at New York State Fair, Syracuse, N. Y.

The
GOLDEN AGE
OF
ONONDAGA LAKE
RESORTS

DONALD H. THOMPSON

Donald H. Thompson

PURPLE MOUNTAIN PRESS
FLEISCHMANNS, NEW YORK

The Golden Age of Onondaga Lake Resorts

First edition 2002

Published by
Purple Mountain Press, Ltd.
P.O. Box 309, Fleischmanns, New York 12430-0309
845-254-4062, 845-254-4476 (fax), purple@catskill.net
http://www.catskill.net/purple

ISBN 1-930098-36-7
Library of Congress Control Number: 2002112014

5 4 3 2 1
Manufactured in the United States of America on acid-free paper

CONTENTS

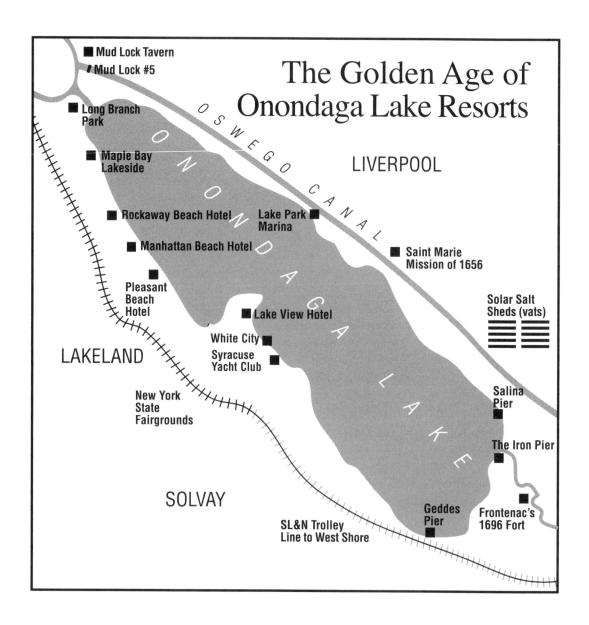

The Golden Age of Onondaga Lake Resorts

Mud Lock Tavern

Mud Lock #5

Long Branch Park

Maple Bay Lakeside

LIVERPOOL

Rockaway Beach Hotel

Lake Park Marina

Manhattan Beach Hotel

Saint Marie Mission of 1656

Pleasant Beach Hotel

Solar Salt Sheds (vats)

Lake View Hotel

White City

LAKELAND

Syracuse Yacht Club

New York State Fairgrounds

Salina Pier

The Iron Pier

SOLVAY

Geddes Pier

Frontenac's 1696 Fort

SL&N Trolley Line to West Shore

OSWEGO CANAL

ONONDAGA LAKE

PREFACE

There seems to be a gap in the knowledge of most people currently living in Central New York regarding the rich history of the west shore of Onondaga Lake. It is ironic that so many of us are familiar with the history of the east shore, thanks to the make-work Depression era projects such as the Ste. Marie Mission to the Haudenosaunee (Iroquois) and the Salt Museum, but we know nothing about the many resorts that existed along the west shore. The purpose of this book is to create an appreciation for the great number of resorts that once lined the west shore. Only the Haley West Shore Trail crosses the resorts' location today, and the surrounding land has almost completely reverted back to a natural state. It was the west shore that was developed as a resort community in the nineteenth century, while the east shore was almost completely undeveloped.

During the 1930s, the east shore was transformed from marshland and thousands of deteriorating solar salt sheds, to the Onondaga County Park, which stretched from Syracuse to Liverpool. Ever since Syracuse's first mayor in 1847, politicians have dreamed of making a park around the entire lake, but this has never been achieved in spite of plans to do so during the 1920s, 1950s, and later. Politicians and planners are again trying to bring a renaissance to Onondaga Lake as a recreational playground, similar to its heyday in the late-nineteenth and early-twentieth centuries.

It is my hope that people who read this book will appreciate the uniqueness, variety, and the sheer number of recreational attractions once available along the lake. It contains funny anecdotes and sometimes sad stories about the people who traveled by steamer or trolley car to enjoy the amusement parks at White City, Pleasant Beach, Maple Bay, or Long Branch Park. For a time during the 1890s, the Iron Pier was the "gateway" to the west shore resorts via lake steamers that would go first to Lake View Point and then on to the other resorts up the lake. As the trolley lines expanded their service along the west shore, the companies built attractions like the Rustic Theater at Maple Bay and later the White City Amusement Park. These attractions were very popular for a time and increased the number of riders for the trolley line. At the turn of the century these lakeshore resorts were at the height of their popularity, but the effects of water pollution by the Solvay Process Company, the city sewage system, and others helped to convince vacationers to seek recreation somewhere other than Onondaga Lake. Now, after years of neglect, a new generation is trying once again to use Onondaga Lake as a center for recreation as it was used during the "Golden Age of the Onondaga Lake."

I have many people to thank for helping to bring this book to fruition. My most constant supporter in life as well as this book has been my wife, Carol, who has tirelessly proofread and critiqued each and every chapter. Joan Burdick has been my typist par excellence. In gathering information, I would like to thank the local history staff at the Syracuse Public Library, the staff at the research room of the Onondaga Historical Association, Jeoff Socha at the Solvay Public Library, Joyce Mills at the Liverpool Public Library, Dorianne Gutierrez at the Liverpool Historical Association, and Trudy Eiler at the Pine Grove Press. Valerie Bell and Elaine Wisowaty from the Ste. Marie Living History Museum gave me advice on people to contact and allowed me to use their archives. Valerie Bell, Kathleen Beardsley, and Anne Skinner have spent hours proofreading the following text. I would like to thank the following Onondaga County officials for their encouragement: John Cooley, Nicholas Pirro, and Robert Geraci. Former Tram Tour guide Walter Schmidt shared the information he had compiled for his tours of Onondaga Lake.

Because of his expertise on local history, I sought the advice of columnist Dick Case many times. I have endeavored to obtain as much firsthand and primary source information as possible, particularly through interviews of people who lived through some part of the "Golden Age of Onondaga Lake Resorts." I especially enjoyed talking to Mildred Leib and Eugene Lee, who at the time of the interview were both 102 years old. I was fortunate enough to meet Kermit Maurer at the last moment; he is the grandson of one of the founders of Long Branch Park. Their recollections of days gone by have been invaluable. I thank the following people for sharing their experiences: Kenneth Lang, Helen Busher, Betty Henes, Howard Hurst, Rose Feikert, Joan Gleason Fichett, James Duerr, and John Maurer. I was especially fortunate to meet June Hecker, the wife of George Hecker, one of the owners of the Rockaway Beach Resort. She kindly shared with me some old photos of the Hecker brothers. I would also like to thank the historian of the Onondaga Yacht Club, Gary Klink, who also shared old photographs. As a result of hearing about my project in a Dick Case column, Dave Oster shared his expertise on historic roller coaster designs and other amusement rides. Tod Weseloh loaned one-of-a-kind photographs of activities at Long Branch Park, and Richard Barnes donated old pictures to the Office of Museums at Onondaga County Parks. I am grateful to Patricia Conway for sharing her souvenir booklets of the Ka Noo No Karnival and to Margaret Valerino for sharing information on the 1943 Solvay sludge flood. Boberetta Johnson Albrigo shared her memories of working with her grandfather, Robert Johnson, at Pleasant Beach. Anne Grovine told about her experience with Camp Syracuse. Without the support of these people with links to the past, this book would not have been made possible.

I wish to thank the following people for helping me gather a variety of historic and present-day maps of Onondaga Lake: Liz Sheets, Hugh Canham, Paul Shemko, and Joe Sallin. Many thanks to Mike Vecellio for the hours he spent scanning over 120 illustrations and burning them into a CD. Most of the illustrations are from my personal postcard collection, but others are thanks to the cooperation of the Onondaga Historical Association and the archives at Onondaga County Parks. I would like to thank my sons, Andrew Thompson, for providing sketches of events in the 1890s, and Bryan Thompson, for helping with maps and generating a website for this book. Thanks also to Mike Spencer for doing the map work, to Gordon DeAngelo for his advice on historic maps, and Theresa Russo for her sketch.

To all of these people and so many others, especially Wray and Loni Rominger and their staff at Purple Mountain Press who gave me encouragement, thank you for making this book possible.

D.H.T.
Winter 2001-2002

CHRONOLOGIES

12,000 Years Ago	Glacial Lake Iroquois covers plain from Rochester to Rome, New York.
1300-1450	The Peacemaker Hiawatha ends intertribal warfare. The Iroquois Confederacy of Five Nations is formed.
1615	Champlain and Huron allies attack Onondaga Village.
1654	French Jesuit Priest Simon LeMoyne is shown salt springs by Onondagas.
1656-1658	The French mission, Ste. Marie, lasts less than two years.
1696	Count de Frontenac invades land of the Onondagas.
1754-1763	The French and Indian War expels France from the east coast of North America.
1768	Treaty of Fort Stanwix prohibits English settlement west of the Appalachian Mountains.
1775	Two runaway black slaves record making salt by salt springs.
1775-1783	The American Revolutionary War
1788	Treaty of Fort Stanwix, land grants are given to Revolutionary War soldiers for their services. Native American claims are restricted to land set aside for reservations. Veterans Comfort Tyler and Asa Danforth first make salt from salt springs.
1793	Beginning of commercial salt production from salt springs.
1822	Onondaga Lake is lowered for drainage of swamps.
1828-1918	The Oswego Canal is built to carry salt and fuel along the east shore of the lake.
1841	The New York State Agricultural Society holds first State Fair in Syracuse.
1847	The first mayor of Syracuse envisions a park around Onondaga Lake.

1862	Nine million bushels of salt are produced, the peak year of the Syracuse Salt Industry.
1871	Captain Fred Ganier navigates steamer to Lake View Point for chowder parties during the summer.
1872	Lake View Point becomes first of the Onondaga Lake Resorts.
1874	Cowan's Grove becomes second lake resort; later its name is changed to Pleasant Beach, the best swimming beach on the lake.
1882	Ben and George Maurer and Frederick Shug purchase land for the Long Branch Resort.
1884	The Solvay Process Company began production of soda ash from salt and limestone.
1888	The Peoples Railroad begins construction of the 50 by 600 feet 'Iron Pier' made out of wood.
1889	Willis E. Barnum purchases land for the Maple Bay Resort, later called Lakeside Resort.
1890	The Manhattan Beach Hotel opens.
	The New York State Fair is permanently located on the shores of Onondaga Lake.
1891	Aeronaut daredevil De Ive falls to his death from a balloon off shoreline at Pleasant Beach.
1892	Civil War vet, Captain John Hecker purchases land from the Cowans for construction of the Rockaway Resort.
1896	Backyard privies are prohibited in Syracuse; sewers now dump waste directly into creeks flowing into Onondaga Lake.
1898	The Syracuse Yacht Club is formed, and a massive clubhouse is built on west the shore across from steel company.
1899	The Syracuse, Lakeshore and Baldwinsville (SL&B) Railroad extended trolley service to Long Branch Park and to Baldwinsville.
	The SL&B railroad opens the Rustic Theater, just south of Maple Bay.
	At the Rustic Theater, "Pain, the Fireworks King" held a spectacular fireworks display commemorating U.S. victory in the Spanish American War.
1900	The Onondaga Lake Ice Yacht Club is formed at the Rockaway Hotel.
1901	The end of ice harvesting on most of Onondaga Lake because of pollution.
1904	Three men are killed in iceboat collision on lake.

1905	The Ka-Noo-No Karnival is held every night during Fair Week to encourage visitors to stay in Syracuse.
1906	The Syracuse, Lakeshore and Northern(SL&N) Railroad builds White City Amusement Park to increase riders on their trolley line.
1907	The Iron Pier fades into history.
	Solvay Process waste is now being dumped on the west shore of the lake, eventually reaching a height of eighty feet.
1909	The SL&N trolley line is extended to Fulton, and, in 1911, to Oswego.
1912	The tornado of September 15, destroys much of Long Branch Park, and kills two men on park grounds.
1915	White City Amusement Park fades into history after only nine years.
	Lake View Point is closed and the city of Syracuse begins proceedings to build a sewage treatment plant.
	A new dam at Phoenix raises the level of Onondaga Lake, requiring the Rockaway Hotel to be moved back 400 feet.
1917	The large wooden Syracuse Yacht Club burns to waterline on May 10.
	The New York State Fairgrounds becomes Camp Syracuse to train horses and soldiers for World War I.
1918	The Oswego Canal is abandoned.
1926	The carousel now at Carousel Mall arrives at Long Branch Park.
	Thomas Gale Jr. was the last of the solar salt barons; the salt industry comes to an end after 138 years.
1928	Joseph Griffin proposes a plan for the park around Onondaga Lake.
1930	Trolley service to lakeshore resorts is discontinued.
	The Onondaga County Work Relief Bureau, led by Crandall Melvin,employs over two thousand men building Onondaga Lake Park, including the Salt Museum, Ste. Marie Mission, and the Jesuit Well, and rebuilding the Mud Lock #5 on the Oswego Canal.
1933	Danforth Salt Swimming Lake, 700 by 150 feet, is completed on southeast shoreline.
1938	Long Branch Park closes after half a century.
1940	Swimming in Onondaga Lake is banned.
1941	The Long Branch carousel is sold to Roseland Park in Canandaigua.
1943	An eight-foot wall of Solvay Process waste floods the State Fairgrounds, after breaking a retaining wall.

1946	Mercury waste is discharged directly into the lake by Allied Chemical (Solvay Process Co.).
1950	One hundred and thirty-nine industries now use Onondaga Lake as a waste basin.
1952	Onondaga Lake becomes site of Intercollegiate Spring Rowing Regatta.
1953	The state drops damage claims against Solvay Process for 1943 spill in return for 400 acres of waste beds to build Route 690 and State Fair parking lots.
1954	Both Rockaway and Pleasant Beach Hotels are destroyed to make way for Route 690.
1955	Planning Board makes plans for creation of lagoons on west shore.
1960's	The Environmental Protection Agency establishes rigid standards for waste deposits.
1979	New Metropolitan Sewage Treatment Plant is built on south shore of lake.
2000	Latest plan to bring about a renaissance of the lake. Recreational trails will "loop the lake" and link up with creek walk next to the new Inner Harbor and other trails.
	Old Barge Canal Terminal will be transformed into a pedestrian promenade around the harbor, and an amphitheater will be built into the hill on the west side of the harbor.
2002	Destiny USA, expansion of present Carousel Mall begins construction.

CHAPTER 1
A GEOLOGICAL AND HISTORIC OVERVIEW
OF ONONDAGA LAKE BEFORE THE RESORT ERA

Onondaga Lake, elevation 370 feet, is part of the Oswego River drainage basin that flows into Lake Ontario. Today the lake is approximately 4.6 miles long and has a maximum width of one mile, much smaller than it was prior to 1822, when the lake was lowered about two feet to allow development of the marshland along the south end of the lake. At the beginning of the twenty-first century, one unique feature of Onondaga Lake is that eighty percent of the shoreline is parkland, with most of it owned by Onondaga County. Another more infamous characteristic of Onondaga Lake today is that it is one of the most polluted lakes in the United States. None of the above facts about Onondaga Lake were true in the past!

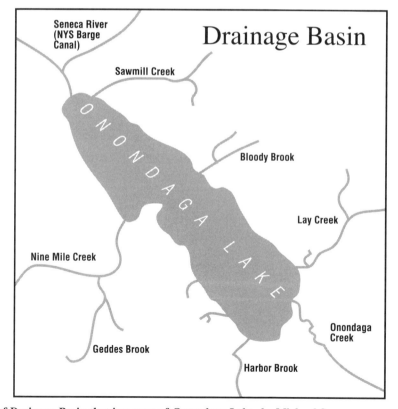

1.1 Map of Drainage Basin that is a part of Onondaga Lake, by Michael Spencer.

In the Beginning

During the Silurian Period, about 430 million years ago, salt beds were formed. These salt beds created Syracuse's salt industry much later. The surface of the land extending from present-day New York to Michigan sank, allowing the sea to encroach and form a large salty inland sea. Later, mountains arose to the east, and this inland sea gradually evaporated, leaving salt formations hundreds of feet thick. Over many millennia, the accumulation of dead marine animals and mud produced fossil-filled limestone and sandstone over the salt layers. The gradual erosion of the higher lands to the east brought shale, silt, and clay deposits.

At least two, but possibly as many as four, separate ice invasions swept over the central part of New York, with the last glacier advancing south around twenty-five thousand years ago, and lasting until about ten thousand years ago. As this mile-high glacier inched forward, it gouged the land surface creating lakes and basins. Glacial Lake Iroquois, the forerunner of Lake Ontario, was formed by the huge glaciers that gouged the landscape like a mammoth bulldozer and filled the holes with water as the climate warmed and the glaciers retreated north. Lake Iroquois was much larger than present-day Lake Ontario, covering all of the lake plain from Rochester to Rome, including what is now Onondaga Lake.

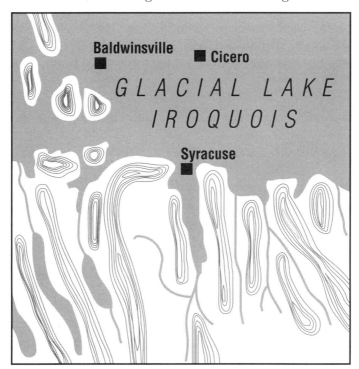

1.2 Map showing extent of Glacial Lake Iroquois, by Michael Spencer.

As the last glacier retreated, it deposited great quantities of silt, sand, and gravel into the valleys, forming natural dams, and creating the Finger Lakes. Onondaga Lake would have extended farther south to what is today the Onondaga Indian Reservation if the sediment-laden Onondaga Creek had not filled in the trough that included what is now the city of Syracuse.

About ten thousand years ago, the first human occupation of North America began when small groups of hunters and gatherers moved across the area in search of food. It was not until CE (Common Era, equivalent of AD) 1000, at the beginning of the Late Woodland stage of Native American development, that there was an increasing trend toward year-round occupation of a site. Gradually, the Indian villages became larger and more stable with the introduction of maize, or corn, as a staple crop.

The native oral tradition records that Hiawatha, an Onondaga; 'the "Peacemaker," a Huron; and Mother of Nations, a Seneca clanmother, ended a bloody period of intertribal warfare among the Iroquois and established the Great Peace, by forming the Iroquois Confederacy of Five Nations. Hiawatha gave the speeches because the Peacemaker stammered, or maybe was not fluent in the language because he was a Huron. Oral tradition recognized the northeastern shore of Onondaga Lake as the scene of the founding of the Iroquois Confederacy. Based on their findings, archaeologists believe that the confederacy was formed sometime during the fifteenth century, prior to European contact. This mutual nonaggression agreement appears to have fostered trade, based upon the existence of artifacts made from copper or shell, which were not found locally.

Tradition holds that at Hiawatha Point on Onondaga Lake, the first Grand Council of Sachem Chiefs accepted the Great Law of Peace, recording the event on a wampum belt. The Onondaga Nation became known as the Keepers of the Council Fire because of their central location. Their main village was south of present-day Syracuse where the Iroquois Confederacy of Five Nations held their council meetings.

On the south shore of Onondaga Lake at the mouth of Onondaga Creek is the only pre-colonial Iroquois fishing village site located on the lake. Dr. William G. Hinsdale, an amateur archaeologist from Syracuse, called the village "Kaneeda," possibly an Anglicism of Ganuutaah. During the summer of 1893, Dr. Hinsdale found a large quantity of artifacts, just before the city of Syracuse began using it as a dump, and later Solvay refuse was dumped on the site of Kaneeda. He found, "Iroquois pottery in fragment form, upon some of which are human faces. . .net sinkers, flakes, split bones of deer, cracked stones, a few wrought flints. In addition, shell beads and a small rectangular piece of utilized scrap brass."[1] Kaneeda Village possibly was the same fortified fishing village attacked by Champlain's forces in 1615, but more will be explained about this on a subsequent page.

The Seventeenth Century French and Dutch Contacts with Onondaga Lake
During the 1600s, the French were among the first Europeans to trade metal tools and colorful glass beads with the Onondaga tribe in return for beaver pelts used to make fashionable felt hats. The Dutch and later the English, traded with the Iroquois, especially the Mohawk Nation, closest to their settlements along the Hudson River. Unknowingly, the French alliance with the Hurons to secure beaver pelts quickly brought them into armed conflict with the Iroquois, the enemies of the Hurons. On three occasions Samuel

de Champlain was asked to accompany Huron raids on the Iroquois nations of the Mohawk and Onondaga. In the fall of 1615 Champlain was the first known European to enter Onondaga territory when he unsuccessfully attacked a fortified Onondaga fishing village, thought at first to be Kaneeda, near the present site of the Carousel Mall.

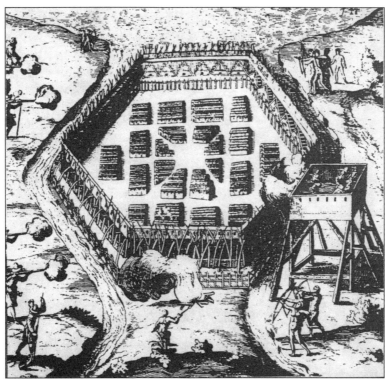

1.3 Drawing of Samuel de Champlain's 1615 attack on Fortified Onondaga Fishing Village, from Onondaga Co. Parks, Office of Museums.

According to the latest archaeological evidence, it is believed that, "the 'fort' attacked by Champlain was on Nichols Pond in Madison County,"[2] not on the banks of Onondaga Lake. Wherever the conflict occurred, it lasted six days and Champlain was left unable to walk, with two arrow wounds to his leg. In his notes of the skirmish, Champlain mentions that the Onondaga had received some assistance from the Dutch who were already trading with them by 1615. It would not be until 1634 that surviving Dutch records note a party of three men visiting a large Oneida town with the purpose of increasing the fur trade at Fort Orange (Albany). The Oneida and a delegation of ten Onondaga were not impressed with what the Dutch offered for the beaver pelts, so the Dutch returned to Fort Orange without a trade agreement with the Iroquois.

By the mid-seventeenth century, the Iroquois had conquered the French allies, the Huron Nation, and were now in a position to control the fur trade with the French. At first they started to attack French settlements in the St. Lawrence River Valley, but then the Onondaga called for a truce because they didn't want to fight the Eries and the French simultaneously. But more important, the Onondaga wanted an easier way of trading with the Europeans, instead of going through the Mohawk to the east. Because of this desire, in 1653, the Onondaga requested that the French send the 'black robes,' Jesuit priests, among their people in hopes of trading furs with them for metal implements and trade beads.

Father Simon LeMoyne, a Jesuit missionary, was chosen to make the peace treaty because he had worked with the Iroquois before. After almost a month of traveling on the rivers and lakes between Quebec and Onondaga Lake, in August 1654, Father LeMoyne was taken to the main Onondaga village at Indian Hill near Pompey. During his first visit to Onondaga Lake, the Onondaga showed Father LeMoyne a spring, the water of which they refused to drink, claiming it was bitter. Father LeMoyne soon surmised that the water was salty, even though they were hundreds of miles from the ocean. He instructed the Indians to boil the water, evaporating the brine and leaving behind salt crystals, a substance the French used to keep their food edible. He was so impressed with the results that he took salt samples back to Quebec.

In 1932, a stone memorial was constructed by the Onondaga County Public Works Administration on the site of a nineteenth century salt well to commemorate Father Simon LeMoyne's discovery of the salt springs in 1654. The Gale Salt Spring is located on the Onondaga Lake Parkway, just before you reach Route 81 going into Syracuse. This memorial is in the area where Father LeMoyne was shown the salt springs in 1654.

1.4 **The Gale Salt Spring along Onondaga Lake Parkway, Syracuse, N.Y., postcard published by Wm. Jubb Co. Syracuse, N.Y., no postmark, author's collection.**

In July 1656, fifty Frenchmen returned to the banks of Onondaga Lake to build a mission called Sainte Marie among the Iroquois in honor of the Virgin Mary. Father LeMoyne, after his visit in 1654 to the Onondaga, apparently never came to the Ste. Marie Mission; at least no written records have survived to confirm his presence at the mission. There were seven Jesuits, twelve soldiers, and the remaining majority were craftsmen, workers, and *donnés*. The *donnés* were often young and always single men who worked for free in return for food and lodging. The *donnés* were unique to New France, as they took the same vows as the priests, but for a limited term; some kept renewing their vows for a lifetime.

The French brought chickens and pigs and augmented their meat supply with fishing and hunting. Onondaga Lake and its tributaries provided a ready supply of eels, salmon, trout, bass, and many other fish, and wild animals were attracted to the salt licks around the salt springs.

For twenty months the mission operated like a "little European town" with its variety of craftsmen and self-sufficiency. With its vegetable garden, domesticated animals, and abundant supply of nearby fish and game, the mission was well provided with food. At the Ste. Marie Among the Iroquois Mission, a stockade, chapel, and a workhouse were erected. Outside the stockade, a large field was laid out not far from Onondaga Lake, for the cultivation of turnips, wheat, beans, squash, and herbs.

1.5 The present replica of the Ste. Marie Among the Iroquois Mission, taken 1999, Onondaga Co. Parks, Office of Museums.

The Mohawk, who were not directly threatened by the Erie, wished to maintain their trade monopoly with the Dutch and pushed to end the truce with France. With the defeat of the Erie in 1657, the peaceful relationship between the French and Iroquois deteriorated rapidly. In late winter of 1658, an

Onondaga convert to Christianity advised the French that the Iroquois no longer welcomed the small mission, and the French, who were isolated from any hope of reinforcements, chose to leave.

The well-known voyageur Pierre Radisson devised a plan to secretly construct boats to prepare for escape on Onondaga Lake. As the boats were being built, they were concealed under the floorboards of the mission. The French prepared large quantities of food and invited the Onondaga to a large feast on March 20, 1658. The Onondaga, after feasting and playing games for three solid days without rest, retired a short distance from the Ste. Marie Mission.

Did the Iroquois know what was going on at the feast? It was not typical of the Iroquois to attack people they had invited, so possibly the Iroquois were glad to see the French leave as relations deteriorated. The French swiftly and silently paddled away in their newly constructed boats as the Iroquois slept, arriving safely in Montreal about two weeks later. Only passing visits by French priests, fur traders and Count de Frontenac's attack in 1696 occurred over the next century, with Europeans not settling along the shore of Onondaga Lake until after the American Revolution.

In 1933, as part of the Onondaga County Public Works Project, a replica of the Ste. Marie Mission to the Iroquois was built to commemorate the first European attempt to establish a settlement in what became Central New York State. The 1933 replica was both inaccurate and misplaced, but in 1975 the mission was reconstructed to conform more accurately to the configuration of the original mission. The photo that follows shows cars driving along the newly completed Onondaga Lake Parkway and a parking lot on the south side of the mission. The caption on the 1950s postcard that follows describes Ste. Marie as a fort, and claims it is a true reproduction rebuilt from Jesuit plans, thus giving a whole generation of Central New Yorkers the erroneous idea that Ste. Marie was primarily a fortification, instead of a mission.

1.6 Replica of the Ste. Marie Mission, with public entrance on south side of 'fort,' 1933, Onondaga Co. Parks, Office of Museums.

1.7 Postcard of Fort Sainte Marie De Gannentaha, Lusterchrome by Tichnor Bros., Inc., Boston, Massachusetts, no postmark, author's collection.

The actual site of the mission today lies beneath LeMoyne Manor Restaurant. On a 1797 map of Onondaga Lake, a mysterious stockade was drawn in by James Geddes in the location of today's restaurant. Archaeological excavations done during the summers of 1974 and 1979 uncovered a small number of artifacts that point to a mid-seventeenth century occupation, and a series of post molds, round organic stains, indicate the physical evidence of either a fortified palisades or a building wall of the original Ste. Marie Mission. The most recent replica includes a chapel, blacksmith shop, carpenter's shop, cookhouse, and living quarters. Ste. Marie now has a "living history" program; costumed staff portray members of the French mission and perform crafts and chores of the mid-seventeenth century.

The French again returned to Onondaga Lake during the summer of 1696, when the governor of New France, Count de Frontenac, launched a devastating invasion of the region. He assembled an army of about two thousand, and used four hundred boats to transport his forces from Montreal up the St. Lawrence into Lake Ontario and up the Oswego River. He entered Onondaga Lake on August 1, 1696, after about four weeks of travel, mostly upstream. The French forces then constructed a fortification at a point that is today Hiawatha Boulevard, near the end of Pulaski Street. In 1696, the fort was located on the south shore of Onondaga Lake, but the site is now 1,200 feet from the current edge of the lake, due to the lowering of the lake in 1822, and the extensive use of Solvay Process waste material to fill in surrounding marshlands.

From this fortification on the south shore, the French marched inland to destroy the main Onondaga village, but the Onondaga tribe had already burned and abandoned their village before their arrival. "The French spent several days destroying fields of crops and stored grain, and sent a detachment under Chevalier de Vaudrueil to destroy the crops of an Oneida Village."[3] In the end, the Iroquois suffered little loss, but the lasting effect of this invasion was to further cement their alliances with the English, effectively preventing the return of the French to Central New York.

The British built a garrison at Oswego and a trading house on the west side of the river in 1722. The French maintained a fort at Niagara, but would not return to Central New York until 1756, when Louis Joseph de Montcalm's forces captured Fort Ontario at Oswego. When the French failed to gain a decisive victory at Battle Island just north of Fulton, they withdrew, and the British rebuilt the garrison at Oswego. Just before the French and Indian War of the mid eighteenth century, "In 1751, the British agent, Sir William Johnson, had bought up all the land around Onondaga Lake for $15,000. . . . He had heard rumors that the French wanted to control the salt springs and this worried him. Since the British had lost the Revolutionary War, the original sale to Johnson was nullified."[4]

The Iroquois Loss of Land

During the period between 1650 and 1776 the Iroquois Nation, through treaties, almost always sided with the British in their struggle with the French for control of North America. During the American Revolution, the Iroquois Nation was split in their allegiance, with the Mohawk favoring the British and the Oneida the Americans. The Mohawk warrior Joseph Brant participated in the siege of Fort Stanwix in 1777 and led a raid on Cherry Valley the following year, massacring many of its inhabitants before marching west through Onondaga lands.

During the spring and summer of 1779, General George Washington approved of a campaign to teach a lesson to the Iroquois who were sympathetic to the British. Over five hundred American soldiers led by Colonel Goose Van Schaick traveled across Oneida Lake from Fort Stanwix to Fort Brewerton, and then on to Onondaga Lake the next day. "At Onondaga Creek they slipped across a log bridge near the present location of West Colvin Street. There they captured a young Indian who provided them with information about the tribe's whereabouts—[by one account] this skirmish was reportedly where lower Onondaga Park stands today. However, according to historian William Beauchamp, General John Sullivan never came into Onondaga territory, and Van Schaick is given full credit for destroying the village just south of where Seneca turnpike and Onondaga Creek now cross."[5]

During the mid-eighteenth century, traders, missionaries, and explorers visited the Onondaga, learning of the salt springs around Onondaga Lake. During 1775, it was recorded, "that two black men, escaped slaves from Ulster County, were engaged in the manufacture of salt."[6] In 1768, in order to keep peace with the Iroquois before the American Revolution, the British government established a line of demarcation in the Treaty of Fort Stanwix that prohibited settlement west beyond the source of the rivers in the Appalachian Mountains. In the Treaty of Fort Stanwix, 1788, after the Revolution, all Iroquois title to land was extinguished except for 7,300 acres of land south of

Syracuse that was reserved for the Onondaga and 400 acres south of Oneida that went to the Oneida Nation. The rest of Central and Western New York was parceled out in land grants to the American Revolutionary soldiers as bounty for their services.

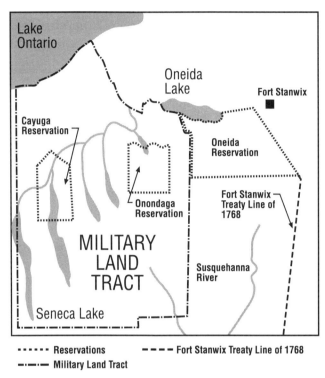

1.8 Map of military land tract of Central New York, by Michael Spencer.

Many of the war veterans never came to claim their land, but sold it to land speculators instead. One of the earliest settlers was Ephraim Webster, who set up a trading post near the mouth of Onondaga Creek. His accounts of his successful trade with the Onondaga Nation encouraged war veteran Asa Danforth to come in 1788. During this same year Comfort Tyler, another Revolutionary War veteran, claimed his land near Onondaga Lake, and in time, the Onondaga showed him the salt springs along the lake. He boiled down the brine in a large iron kettle over a fire and continued to make salt crystals in this fashion for his own use. Soon Comfort Tyler and Asa Danforth were working together, boiling down the brine to make salt used for preserving fish and meat. These two Revolutionary War veterans were the start of the Syracuse salt industry that would become a major economic activity along the shores of Onondaga Lake for 100 years.

Growth of the Salt Industry

Soon settlers like Nathaniel Loomis made salt using as many as fifteen kettles at a time and sold it for one dollar a bushel. Later, settlers developed a "salt block," with iron kettles held in a stone foundation over a fire. Moses DeWitt then refined the process by using gravity-fed wooden troughs to fill the iron kettles. As long as the wood supply from the surrounding area remained plentiful, the boiling system was used.

During the first half of the nineteenth century, a total of 316 salt blocks were built next to the Oswego and Erie Canals that ran along parts of both shores of Onondaga Lake. The chimney of Jacqueth/VanAlstine 'Salt Block 56' is the only lasting physical structure saved from the Salt Era, as it was incorporated into the Salt Museum in 1933. This old photo shows workers building the Salt Museum, using old timbers from Thomas Gale's salt warehouse. The chimney shown was built in 1856, when fuel to boil the brine was still inexpensive.

1.9 Photo showing construction of the Salt Museum, 1933, Onondaga Co. Parks, Office of Museums.

The Oswego Canal was constructed by 1829, between the Erie Canal and Lake Ontario, to provide a cheap form of transportation. It brought wood south for the "salt blocks" furnaces and shipped barrels of salt to markets in the Midwest and Canada. Some of the salt blocks had as many as sixty iron kettles. The brine was piped in through miles of wooden pipes from the state-owned Salt Springs Reservation pump houses. Between 1797-1908, New York State took over the land around the southern end of Onondaga Lake to prevent any one person from creating a salt monopoly, and the state levied a tax on each barrel of salt to pay for construction of the Erie and Oswego Canals.

During the peak year of 1862, over 9 million bushels of salt were produced around Onondaga Lake. After the Civil War the price of coal soared, encouraging the building of solar evaporation sheds by the thousands to produce salt cheaper. As many as 43,000 sheds were built so the brine would evaporate by the combined strength of the sun and wind. When it rained a bell was rung, and hundreds of school children and workers would rush out to pull wooden covers over the evaporation beds so the brine would not be diluted, setting back the evaporation process.

By 1887, Thomas Gale had become the "Solar Salt King of Onondaga," owning 5,000 evaporation beds and several large storehouses. This old post-card, sent in 1909, shows the extent of the Gale solar salt evaporation beds in what is today Galeville, overlooking Onondaga Lake. The second picture shows the hundreds of solar evaporation sheds next to Onondaga Creek in the vicinity of Spencer Street. The north side skyline of Syracuse can be seen in the distance, including Assumption Catholic Cathedral.

1.10 Postcard of solar salt covers, Syracuse, N.Y., published by American Publicity Co., Syracuse, N.Y., postmarked 1909, author's collection.

1.11 Solar salt sheds near Spencer Street on Syracuse's North side, Onondaga Co. Parks, Office of Museums.

By the end of the nineteenth century, the Syracuse salt industry was competing with rival salt companies farther west that did not have to go through the lengthy process of evaporating brine. Thomas Gale Jr., the last surviving salt producer, finally closed down his salt operations in 1926 after a devastating hurricane destroyed many of the solar salt sheds, effectively ending 138 years of salt production around Onondaga Lake. Mr. Gale donated salt making equipment and the timbers of one of his salt warehouses for construction of the Salt Museum.

The Oswego Canal was abandoned in 1918, but it was not until the Onondaga Lake Park was created in the early 1930s, that the canal was filled with garbage, and Route 370, the Onondaga Lake Parkway, was built over the top of the canal. This old photograph was taken just south of the low railroad bridge looking towards Syracuse. When this picture was taken, some of Thomas Gale's salt warehouses were still standing on the east side of the parkway.

1.12 Onondaga Lake Parkway showing Gale's Salt Warehouses, circa early 1930s, Onondaga Co. Parks, Office of Museums.

The part of the Oswego Canal between the Salt Museum and the old Oswego Canal Mud Lock has now become the East Shore Trail next to Onondaga Lake, where hundreds get their daily exercise walking, jogging, or rollerblading.

After the Civil War, before the pollution of the lake during the late-nineteenth century, the "Golden Era of Onondaga Lake Resorts" began. In 1872,

Fred Ganier built the Lake View Point Resort, which could be reached by steamers traveling over Onondaga Lake. Before the end of the century at least eight resorts were built along Onondaga Lake, the majority of which were on the west shore. The subsequent chapters will explore the rise and decline of these resorts and include contemporary photos, news articles, and personal interviews, beginning first with the Iron Pier on the southeast shore of the lake and ending with Long Branch Park on the north shore of the lake. The story of these very popular resorts, which brought a surprisingly large number of leisure activities to Central New York, is unfamiliar to many people today, as the west side of the lake has reverted to undergrowth and woods, and its access by the public is restricted by Route 690.

Notes

1. James W. Bradley, *Evolution of the Onondaga Iroquois*, from notes for chapter 4 on p. 224, Syracuse University Press, 1987.

2. Bradley p. 224.

3. Walter H. Schmidt, "The 1696 French Fort of Count Frontenac," unpublished notes, 1988.

4. *The Village of Liverpool, N.Y., Its First 150 Years*, Historical Association of Liverpool, p. 3, 1980.

5. Henry W. Schramm, *Central New York, A Picture History*, p. 7, The Donning Co., Norfolk Virginia, 1987.

6. *The Village of Liverpool, N.Y., Its First 150 Years* p. 12.

Chapter 2
The Iron Pier, 1890-1907

The Building of the Iron Pier

On the south shore of Onondaga Lake, close to where the Carousel Shopping Center is located today, a resort called the Iron Pier stood for seventeen years. During the 1890s, trolley companies got into the business of developing resorts along their lines to increase ridership. Before trolleys were electrified, horse drawn cars took people north from Clinton Square to the south end of Onondaga Lake, where passengers would then board a steamer to reach the early resorts on the west shore of the lake. The People's Railway Company of Utica decided this transfer junction from trolley to steamer would be an ideal location to construct a new resort to attract thousands of people. After asking for bids on January 20, 1890, the company hired Horace Hallock to be the contractor to build the Iron Pier, which, by the way, was iron in name only.

When finished, the Iron Pier was a long, narrow wooden pavilion of 50 by 600 feet, situated between the shore and the railroad line, as shown in the Sanborn map of 1892. On the east end of the structure were bowling alleys, and the concert hall was located at the west end. Adjacent was the Salina Pier's Grangers Pavilion that housed a dining room and a concert hall. The Salina Pier was a rival establishment that competed with the Iron Pier for business during the early 1890s.

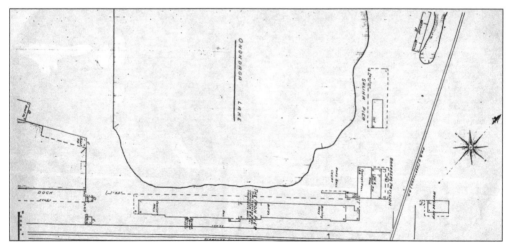

2.1 Sanborn map of 1892 showing south shore of Onondaga Lake and the Iron Pier, Syracuse Public Library microfilm collection of Sanborn maps.

By March 1890, Hallock had the resort well on its way to completion. The *Syracuse Standard* newspaper reported on March 2, 1890, that "the piling is all down, the wharves completed, the channel and harbor nearly all dredged out and the erection of the grand pavilion has been commenced. The place looks like a large shipyard, with its huge piles of lumber and timbers, and three scows on the stocks – one of which is a 90-footer to be used for carrying the marl which is dredged out."[1] Hallock continued to push his large work force, as huge timbers arrived from as far away as Georgia to support the roof of the pavilion.

The People's Railway seemed to face some of the same problems construction projects face today, more than one hundred years later. During the month of April, fishermen were using nets to catch large quantities of game fish at the mouth of Onondaga Creek, close to where the Iron Pier was built. The *Syracuse Standard* of April 7, notes that some fishermen stayed all night with their nets and kept warm with bonfires. "They are not at all particular what goes into the bonfires, and contractor Hallock is compelled to keep a watchman on the new pier all night to prevent them using up the Pavilion."[2]

This old photograph shows a group picture of the many carpenters and laborers who worked on the Iron Pier during the spring of 1890, through all sorts of weather conditions, to complete the pavilion for the start of the summer season. Someone's pet dog must have given a little comic relief during the long work days that spring.

2.2 Carpenters and laborers completing the Iron Pier Pavilion, Spring 1890, Onondaga Historical Association Collection.

The People's Railway Company had further obstacles to a successful and smooth season opening. In June 1890, the rival Salina Pier put up an eight-foot high billboard on their premises in front of the Iron Pier. "The Iron Pier people objected, thinking that it would shut off their view of the lake, and James Farrell, local manager of the pier, made a pilgrimage to the chief of the fire department."[3] In the end, Chief Eckel had the sign removed, but the bitterness between the rival businesses continued all summer. In July, more trouble came in the form of a financial lien against contractor Hallock and the People's Railway for nonpayment for some of the construction materials. One can only speculate that the bill for $7,000 was eventually paid to the C.C. Kellogg of Utica.

Attractions of the Iron Pier

By May 1890, 138 men were still working on the Iron Pier in hopes of a June 1 completion. That spring seemed to usher in a boom time for the Onondaga Lake resort industry, as the rival Salina Pier was completing a two-story pavilion, and Maple Bay was working on a new club house. In spite of the ongoing work around the lake, heavy rains had hampered progress by putting all the piers and groves under as much as three feet of water.

This segment of the 1892 Vose Atlas shows the southern portion of Onondaga Lake closest to Syracuse. Geddes Pier can be seen at the west side of the lake and the long narrow Iron Pier can be seen at the mouth of Onondaga Creek. This map gives more details about the original course of Onondaga Creek as it existed in 1892. This map also shows to the left the straightened manmade version of Onondaga Creek that we know today as the inner harbor.

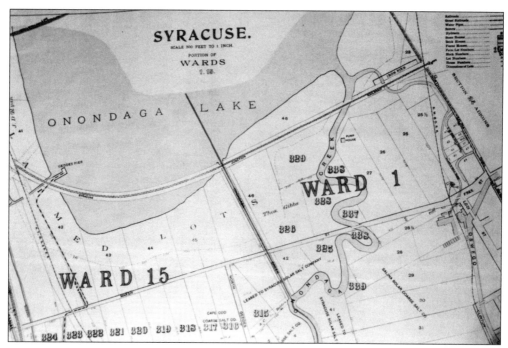

2.3 South shoreline Onondaga Lake Piers, Vose atlas map, 1892, Onondaga Co. Parks, Office of Museums.

Contractor Hallock pushed his men hard every day for completion of the Iron Pier, which was much more than a steamboat terminal. The *Syracuse Standard* of March 2, 1890, reported that, "when the summer season opens Syracuse will have a pleasure resort of which she has been sadly in need."[4] By June 1890, the People's Railway advertised the Iron Pier as a first class family resort, calling it the Coney Island of Central New York. Concerts were given every Monday and Wednesday evenings by the Drescher's Orchestra. Besides concerts, visitors could enjoy bowling alleys, pool and billiard rooms, and outdoor sports.

Even at the end of the summer of 1890, improvements were still being made to the newly built Iron Pier. A stage was erected for the orchestra in the music hall, as well as two very large boathouses. The Iron Pier was considered by many to have the best harbor, from which three steamers embarked every forty-five minutes to resorts on Onondaga Lake.

2.4 The Iron Pier harbor with incoming steamboat, gravure, 1899, Onondaga Historical Association Collection.

It was not until June 30, 1890, that the Onondaga Lake resorts formally opened, due to the high water. By the end of June the weather finally broke, and thousands of people took advantage of the warm sun and breeze to enjoy an outing to the Iron Pier. "Between 2,000 and 8,000 persons visited the Iron Pier, where a band concert was given by Gaylord's Orchestra,"[5] as reported in the June 30 *Syracuse Standard*. In the two-part orchestra program, director Gaylord included two of his own pieces, one of which was the "Iron Pier March." On July 4, 1890, there was a fireworks display that was set off from, "a boat anchored in the harbor, and their reflections on the water made a very novel and pretty effect."[6] By the middle of July, one of the concessions to open up inside the Iron Pier Pavilion was an ice cream parlor selling John F. Rausch's celebrated ice cream, cakes, candies, fruits, and nuts.

During July 1890, the Syracuse chief of police Charles R. Wright warned the Iron Pier not to have any more Sunday music and not to violate the Sunday (blue) laws in relation to the sale of liquor. The People's Railway decided to discontinue the Sunday concerts until further notice. An interesting attraction to take the place of concerts on Sunday, was the creation of a semiprofessional baseball team to be known as the Iron Pier Nine. The field was alongside the pier and up to several hundred fans could sit in the grandstand for free while reserved seats cost five cents. Games were scheduled every day with other area semipro teams such as the Mikados and Maroons. Long Branch Park for a time also had a baseball team, as the game was truly becoming a national sport during this era.

In August 1890, the *Syracuse Standard* reported how extraordinary talent was drawing the greatest crowds of the season every afternoon and evening. It was reported that, "Yank Hoe, the Japanese fantasist from the Crystal Palace, London, and his beautiful Circassian lady assistant, Omene, attracted crowds. . . . Their extraordinary performance is doubling daily the attendance at the Iron Pier."[7] Entertainment manager Farrell scheduled some of the latest and best entertainment for the rest of the season including a favorite Spanish dancer and the Hungarian Gypsy band. The famous Acme Quartet of New York performed in the 327-foot long music hall inside the Pier.

This 1890 color advertisement for the Iron Pier shows the grandeur of the resort. Rail lines and horse drawn cars can be seen transporting people to and from the resort from downtown Syracuse. Once arriving at the Iron Pier, people would board steamboats to reach the thriving resorts on Onondaga Lake's west shore. A round-trip steamer ticket cost fifteen cents. The Pier was the scene of a variety of water sports: sailboat and rowboat rentals, large water toboggan slides, and of course swimming and fishing.

In 1899, the Iron Pier had its grand opening for the season on May 28, starting its tenth year of existence. That day, afternoon and evening concerts were given free of charge to the public, and steamboats left the Pier every forty minutes for a fare of ten cents round-trip, even cheaper than what was charged ten years earlier. In 1899, Charles Demong, the manager of the Iron Pier, inaugurated a season of band concerts at the new Iron Pier Park on high ground north of the main building. The park was designed to seat up to 2,500 people, and concerts were given free every night of the week to patrons of the Rapid Transit Company. The People's Railway had been absorbed into the Syracuse Street Railway in 1894, and the new company acquired the Iron Pier.

On June 20, 1899, because of cool, windy weather, the manager was faced with having the concert inside the pier pavilion or the newly completed park. The next day the *Syracuse Post Standard* reported, "Gaylord's Central City Band was at its best. At times the wind would carry away the sheets of music, but this seemed to make no difference with the players, for they continued to play as though nothing had happened."[8] A crowd of about one thousand people enjoyed the free concert that night. Later in the season elaborate firework displays were added to attract greater numbers to the Iron Pier Park.

2.5 Iron Pier advertisement, 1890 lithograph by Gies and Co., Buffalo. Original image property of Helen Heid Platner, reproduced 1990.

The Iron Pier Becomes a Temperance Park

One problem faced by many Onondaga Lake resorts was the rowdy and sometimes drunken crowds. In an attempt to live up to its earlier advertisement as a first-class family resort, the Rapid Transit System decided to stop selling liquor at the Pier. "By discontinuing the sale of intoxicants on the hundred acres controlled by the railroad company it is hoped so to improve the tone of the resort that our most sensitive citizens will find no objection to patronizing it."[9] In spite of declaring itself a temperance park, big crowds continued to attend the concerts and other attractions at the Pier.

This movement towards making the Pier a temperance resort was something that the long-term manager Charles Demong, and the Rapid Transit System had been scheming for a long time. The Iron Pier had been run strictly since its conception, "but it has gained an unsavory reputation largely because of some dives which have been conducted in the neighborhood. It has been a place where beer was freely sold, and where men and women of all ages have resorted for a free and easy time."[10] In the immediate area around the Iron Pier were hundreds of solar salt vats and nearby salt workers' homes.

One way the Syracuse Street Railway solved this problem was by purchasing adjoining lots to the Pier, until they had 100 acres from the Old Salina Pier to the mouth of Onondaga Creek. The transit company then used Solvay Process soda ash refuse to build up the land in front of the Pier as much as four feet, and then topsoil was placed over the refuse. Trees and shrubs were planted, and water chutes and merry-go-rounds were added to make it a true family 'seaside' resort. For the 1899 season it was decided to discontinue vaudeville performances in the Pier hall and, "in their place Mr. Demong has arranged for a 'biograph show.' He says that the instrument is one of the best made, and that the pictures will be the most popular that can be obtained."[11] A biograph was a trademark for an early type of motion-picture recorder and projector. In 1899, the first silent movies were being made, and it seems that the topics of these movies were better family entertainment than the often more risqué type of comedy used in the vaudeville performances. The same 1899 article ended with: "Mr. Demong stated yesterday that the proposal to furnish a popular resort for the better element in the city, a place where no one would be ashamed to go and take his best friend."[12]

On August 3, 1899, the women's auxiliary of the Young Men's Christian Association held a very successful Iron Pier Day attended by about five thousand people. "The women had complete possession of the big dining hall, and the fact was frequently commented upon that their presence there would go a long way to establish the Iron Pier's new reputation as a temperance resort."[13]

The women's auxiliary received forty percent of the trolley fares that day, and they sold soft drinks, ice cream, cake, popcorn, and peanuts. By the end of the day they made a profit of several hundred dollars and helped to reestablish the Pier's good reputation.

During the afternoon and evening, Gaylord's band of thirty pieces presented a two-part-program. This time Director Gaylord did not include any of his own music, but there were seven pieces written by John Phillip Sousa including, "El Capitan" and "Stars and Stripes."

Almost every day children on summer vacation from school would enter the 100 acres of Iron Pier property to go swimming in Onondaga Lake. Charles N. Winter, who grew up on the north side not far from the Pier, remembered, "All summer we only wore our pants. No shoes or stockings. Our hair was clipped and our feet got tough walking the railroad ties to go swimming in Onondaga Lake near the Iron Pier."[14]

During the early part of the summer of 1899, the Iron Pier had trouble with large numbers of persistent boys attending the open-air concerts at the new temperance park, and leaving their bikes all over the lawn. To solve this problem, a high fence was built, and a policeman was stationed at the new gate to keep out 'wheels' and intoxicated persons. Small boys were allowed entry only if accompanied by an adult. "A number of large racks will be erected today so that all who ride the silent steed to the grounds can have a safe way of disposing of their wheels in the park."[15]

July 4, 1899, was not quite what the Syracuse Street Railway Company had in mind when it planned for record crowds. In spite of rain in the early afternoon and evening, Lakeside trolley cars that went along the west shore and Iron Pier boats carried hundreds to Long Branch, Maple Bay, Rockaway Beach, and Pleasant Beach. The day after the Fourth, the crowds stayed away from the

Onondaga Lake resorts in spite of good summer weather. An article in the July 6 *Syracuse Post Standard* makes a good social commentary about why the masses stayed home. "In the first place there are hundreds of people who make about forty-eight hours out of twenty-four on Independence Day and it cannot be expected that this class of people will make another outing of any description for a week at least. Then, on the other hand, there is a class that makes it a point to spend all its money on the Fourth and it stands to reason that parties doing this must refrain from trolley rides for a few days."[16]

2.6 The Iron Pier before the spring cleanup, 1890s, Onondaga Co. Parks, Office of Museums.

The 1890s picture above shows unsightly trash along the beach in front of the Iron Pier. The Iron Pier pennant is flying briskly over the dome suggesting a strong breeze out of the northwest, that to this day washes up all kinds of debris along the south shoreline.

The End of the Iron Pier

The People's Railway began operating a line from Onondaga Valley to Salina in 1889 and a year later had the Iron Pier built on the south shore of Onondaga Lake to increase ridership on its line. It was designed to be a resort, as well as the junction where steamboats left the Iron Pier for other resorts on the west shore of the Lake. At its height it offered concerts, bowling alleys, a first class restaurant, and various water sports outside the pavilion.

In 1899, the Iron Pier marked its tenth anniversary and had a good year, but that same year the newly-formed Syracuse, Lakeside and Baldwinsville trolley line was extended all the way to Long Branch Park. Now workers and their families could travel to all of the resorts on the west shore of Onondaga Lake without having to take the trolley to the Iron Pier and then the steamboat to the lake resorts. After 1899, weekend vacationers were less interested in enjoying a leisurely boat trip across Onondaga Lake to their favorite resort, than to getting there as rapidly as possible to better enjoy their precious free time. It was previously noted that a round-trip steamboat ticket from the Iron Pier cost less than ten years earlier, possibly the result of competition that eventually cut into profits.

By 1907, the Iron Pier had faded into history, unable to compete successfully with the other Onondaga Lake resorts. Just one year previous to 1907, White City opened at just the first stop out of Syracuse on the competing Syracuse, Lakeside and Baldwinsville trolley line. White City now was the latest investment by a railway company, like its predecessor, the Iron Pier. The glory that went to White City lasted only until 1908 when the park went into receivership. Increasing pollution of Onondaga Lake made the lake less appealing for weekend getaways, encouraging people to take the trolley line to other nearby resorts, such as Oneida Lake. People also began traveling greater distances with the advent of the automobile.

An advertisement in the August 8, 1902, *Syracuse Herald* mentioned that fireworks at the Lake Park (Old Iron Pier) would be postponed until August 11. The Iron Pier Park is shown on this 1908 Hopkins map of the first ward of Syracuse, with nearby land either labeled marsh or soda ash refuse fill. The park itself was built on top of refuse, and the basin was built at the mouth of the original course of Onondaga Creek. This was the same park developed by the Syracuse Street Railway in 1899 to make the Iron Pier a more attractive family resort. The railroad junction

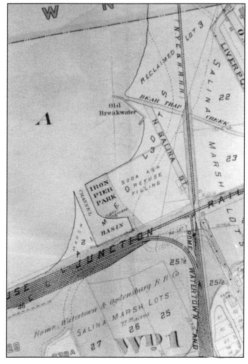

2.7 G.M. Hopkins Co. atlas map of Iron Pier, 1908, Onondaga Co. Parks, Office of Museums.

shown on the map of the southeast corner of Onondaga Lake is still today a center for railroad transportation; the main line passes close by Carousel Mall.

The spot where the Iron Pier was once located has, to a great extent, reverted to its original condition. Across the railroad tracks from Carousel Mall, the land has once again become marshy, in spite of all the fill put in over one hundred years ago to create the recreational park. Cattails thrive and herons now inhabit what was once the finest harbor on Onondaga Lake. This picture shows the spire on the top of Carousel Mall, beyond the trees that have grown up where the Iron Pier once was located.

2.8 **Author's photo of the marsh on the south shore of Onondaga Lake, site of the Iron Pier, Summer 2000.**

Notes

1. "Piers on the Lake," *Syracuse Standard* 2 March 1890.

2. "Pirates Taking Bushels of Fish in Nets," *Syracuse Standard* 7 April 1890.

3. "Rival Saloon-Keepers," *Syracuse Standard* 14 June 1890.

4. "Piers on the Lake."

5. "Along the Lake," *Syracuse Standard* 30 June 1890.

6. "Fizz, Whip, Zip, Boom," *Syracuse Standard* 5 July 1890.

7. "Wonderful Illusions," *Syracuse Standard* 28 August 1890.

8. "No Fear of Chilly Breezes," *Syracuse Post Standard* 21 June 1899.

9. "Elevating The Iron Pier," *Syracuse Post Standard* 16 June 1899.

10. "Downfall of King Booze," *Syracuse Post Standard* 15 June 1899.

11. "Downfall of King Booze."

12. "Downfall of King Booze."

13. "Women Were at the Bar," *Syracuse Post Standard* 4 August 1899.

14. Charles N. Winter, "Letter to the Editor," *Syracuse Post Standard* 30 June 1957.

15. "Large Rocks For Wheels," *Syracuse Post Standard* 22 June 1899.

16. "They Spend Their Coin and the Day Was Dull," *Syracuse Post Standard* 6 July 1899.

3.1 Entrance to the "White City," Syracuse, N.Y., postcard, collection of author.

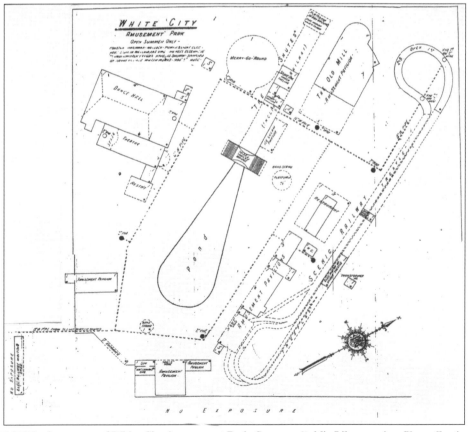

3.2 1910 Sanborn map of White City Amusement Park, Syracuse Public Library microfilm collection.

CHAPTER 3
WHITE CITY

First Stop on the Trolley

In 1906, Onondaga Lake's most spectacular amusement park opened its doors to the public. It was located about five hundred feet north of the present-day entrance to the New York State Fair, on the site of the old Solvay Process waste beds. "The White City Amusement Company issued $80,000 of [*sic*] bonds to build the project. Mr. C. D. Beebe, a trolley magnate, sank $29,000 into the enterprise expecting it to show good profits along with his trolley business."[1] Mr. Beebe was responsible for the development of the Syracuse, Lakeshore and Northern Railway along the west shore of Onondaga Lake, and for just five cents he hoped the masses would come to White City, the first stop out of Syracuse. Mr. F. F. McIver, a builder brought in from New York City who previously had been in charge of the construction of Luna Park at Coney Island, was in charge of constructing White City. The inspiration for the amusement park came from the 1893 Chicago Columbian Exhibition and Luna Park, which is pictured in this c. 1910 postcard showing the Shoot-the-Chutes ride—the center of attraction at White City.

3.3 **Lagoon and Chute the Chutes, Luna Park, published by Braun Post Card Co., Cleveland, Ohio, 1910 postmark, postcard, collection of author.**

The Grand Opening of White City

The new resort was named White City in reference to the prevailing color scheme of the attractions and because of the more than twenty-five thousand electric lights that illuminated it at night. The World's Columbian Exposition of 1893 was held in Chicago as a celebration of the 400th anniversary of Christopher Columbus' arrival in America. The exposition included an enormous Ferris wheel built by Gale Ferris, 250 feet in diameter. Its 36 cars each held up to 60 people for a potential of well over two thousand people per ride. For this historic anniversary the mechanical wonders of the day were housed in buildings made out of plaster and fiber that shone like white marble in the sunlight. Because of this appearance, the exposition was called the White City. After the Columbian Exposition, the name White City became associated with various amusement parks that sprang up in cities across the United States, including Syracuse in 1906.

The construction of White City in Syracuse started in the middle of March, and in order to have things ready for the Memorial Day opening, a great deal of rushing and heroic effort was required. "In a few short months, 150 carpenters and over 350 laborers of the White City Construction Company under F. F. McIver, worked day and night to transform the former pastureland into a sparkling, white

3.4 Full page advertisement in *The Syracuse Post Standard*, **May 19, 1906, "White City, Syracuse Opens Decoration Day, May 30." Syracuse Public Library microfilm collection.**

fantasy land lit with over 25,000 electric lights and complete with its own small lake; a 15,000 square foot ballroom; a first class restaurant overlooking the lake and capable of seating 1,000 people; a Japanese tea garden; a miniature scenic railway; a children's playground; and an open platform with room to seat 5,000 for band concerts and vaudeville performances."[2]

General manager, George F. Kerr, spared no expense for the opening of the amusement park on Decoration (Memorial) Day, May 30, 1906. He took out several full-page ads in the Syracuse newspapers describing some of the thirty amusements and the fabulous free entertainment, and emphasized that the park was only a twelve-minute ride on the trolley from the courthouse on the north side of Clinton Square in Syracuse.

During the opening day, the attendance reached 41,203 by 9:00 PM, just before the fireworks display. In a *Syracuse Post Standard* article the day after the opening, it was reported that, "the transportation capacity of the Syracuse, Lakeshore and Northern Railroad was overtaxed. Every car leaving the courthouse was packed. People were jammed in the vestibules of the closed cars and the running boards and fenders of the open ones. In a number of cases the roofs of the cars were occupied. One car had 211 people, according to the trolley conductor."[3]

Crowds were greeted by the fifty-member Kilties Band from Canada during the first week, playing at the bandstand just beyond the arched entrance. Seats were available for up to 5,000 people. In June, the Duss Band was scheduled to appear, and later in the summer John Phillip Sousa's band was slated to entertain the crowds at White City.

The west side of the grounds included a dance pavilion 100 by 150 feet, with music furnished by a 'large orchestra.' Adjoining the dance pavilion was a theater of oriental design that could seat 500 people. During the first weeks, Miss Lillian Ashley, a well-known comic opera comedienne, was scheduled to perform, and later a variety of vaudeville acts would be presented free of charge at the theater.

The Main Attractions

White City included many amusement rides, but the most popular ride was the Shoot-the-Chutes ride that was found just beyond the entrance gate, in the center of the park grounds. The *Post Standard* on May 31, 1906, reported, "the center of attraction was the Shoot-the-Chutes, and the artificial lake into which the boats plunged was always surrounded by a crowd."[4] For ten cents, or five cents for children, the public could experience a ride like no other around Onondaga Lake. The crowds were impressed by the speed at which the boats careened down the long ramp into the artificial lagoon. Because of its great popularity, more boats were ordered to cut down on long waiting lines.

These two turn-of-the-twentieth-century postcards show the Shoot-the-Chutes ride in the center of White City. The amusement park was built on pastureland sold by W. K. Smith to the trolley magnate, Mr. C. D. Beebe. The view on top of the chute shows the smoke stacks of the steel and soda ash industries in the town of Geddes.

3.5 Shooting the Chutes, White City, Syracuse, N.Y., No. 9, published by William Jubb, Syracuse, N.Y. and Leipzig, made in Germany, collection of author.

3.6 The White City, Syracuse, N.Y., No. 10, published by William Jubb, Syracuse, N.Y., and Leipzig, made in Germany, collection of author.

Rivaling Coney Island in New York City, the scenic railway, built on the east side of the grounds, was billed as the largest in the country. At its peak of ninety feet, thrill seekers had an aerial view above the park overlooking Onondaga Lake, just before rushing down the incline. Unfortunately, the scenic railroad was not in operation opening day because some of the machinery was not yet ready. Once operable, the scenic railway ride was one of the fastest available at the time.

White City boasted many other attractions including, The Temple of Mirth, Airships, Johnstown Flood, Trip to California, and The Old Mill. The Trip to California ride made the rider feel as if he were in a train going across the United States. "The train would shake and a roll of painted scenery would be shown out

3.7 Birds-eye view of "White City," Syracuse, N.Y., postmarked 1906 with special message on front of card, collection of author.

3.8 View of the Scenic Railway at "White City," Syracuse, N.Y., postmarked 1906, room for messge on front of card, not back, collection of author.

the windows to give the feeling of motion."[5] The Old Mill was a boat ride on a canal through tunnels and past a panorama of picturesque scenes. From time to time attractions would change and would include some unusual events such as the "eruption" of Mount Vesuvius, a hippodrome dog and monkey circus, and high wire acts over the artificial lagoon.

When tired of rides and special events, the public could eat at spacious picnic grounds or dine at a first class restaurant and café managed by one of the best restaurant owners in Syracuse. A *Syracuse Journal* article of May 29, 1906, after acclaiming the restaurant, went on to say, "a spacious ballroom with polished maple floors is provided for the devotees of Terpsichore."[6]

One of the novel features of White City was the provision of a free playground for children. In this area of the park, specially trained attendants would care for small children while their parents enjoyed more adult amusements such as the rides or a stroll through the Japanese Tea Garden. A big sand pile was provided for little ones, with pony rides available for older children.

The immense popularity of White City was evident in the trolleys that were full day and night, transporting a constant stream of visitors. Pyrotechnic displays (fireworks) drew large crowds every night. As hundreds arrived from Clinton Square about every ten minutes, others would be awaiting transportation to other west shore resorts, such as Long Branch Park. Many of the other Onondaga Lake resorts also had amusement rides and a variety of live entertainment, so during the height of the resort era just before and after 1900, there was stiff competition to attract customers. One of the techniques used by White City to increase attendance was to form a Children's Club, whose members were admitted free with special buttons. By 1907, the Children's Club had grown to 2,000 members.

3.9 Advertisement, "Admission to White City Absolutely Free," *Syracuse Post Standard*, July 7, 1908, page 4, Syracuse Public Library microfilm collection.

Changing Times

At first, White City charged ten cents for adult admission, but by 1908 they were advertising, "the lid is off, admission to White City is now absolutely free."[7] The advertisement went on to mention that the ride out and back to Syracuse cost only a dime in 1908. With the new free admission policy, crowded cars brought patrons to nightly dances with a live band and all the other attractions at White City. Sets of china and toy balloons were given away as door prizes to further lure the public to White City.

When Mildred Leib was interviewed in 2001 at the age of 102, she was the only person interviewed who could recall going to White City when she was between the ages of seven and nine. She grew up in Syracuse and remembers that once past the Yacht Club, you were almost to White City. Mrs. Leib recalled that after paying admission, you would pass through the entrance arch and immediately see the enormous pool at the base of the Shoot-the-Chutes ride. She mentioned she thought White City didn't last long because the park charged ten cents per ride in addition to admission, a large sum for the early-twentieth century. She has fond memories of going to Long Branch Park with her family. They liked this resort because it had free admission, and there was a greater variety of rides. Nearly every Sunday during the summer her mother would pack a lunch in a market basket, and her father would take them in the family boat up the Oswego Canal, through the Mud Lock to Long Branch Park, where they would have a picnic. Her family was fortunate enough to have had a motorboat that could take them as far as Three Rivers to the north, or east to Dewitt on the Erie Canal, on these Sunday outings.

Even back then, before every family owned an automobile, people wanted to get the most for their recreational dollar, and resort owners were forced to compete with one another to attract the public. Most of the resorts had restaurants, but many families found these too expensive, including Mrs. Leib's, so they preferred picnicking on the picnic grounds provided by Long Branch or other resorts.

George Kerr was the general manager at the opening of the park, hired because of his experience at Coney Island. He hoped to attract at least 400,000 people the first summer, many in excursion groups from towns within a 200 mile radius. His plans included keeping White City open well after dark each night through the season, from late May through September. In the short run, through various promotions, this expectation of large attendance was achieved, as the first two years were an enormous success. However, this initial success was followed by a marked decline in attendance by the third season. "Receivership followed, and the resort was offered for sale in the March 25, 1908, issue of the *Syracuse Journal.* A comeback was attempted several times, without success. Finally, the summer resort for a few years a mecca for outings and excursion parties, folded up. It was torn down in 1915."[8]

The rising popularity of the automobile after World War I meant that families were no longer restricted to the boundaries of the trolley line around Onondaga Lake. White City also lasted for such a relatively brief duration because of its proximity to the ever-expanding Solvay Process waste alkali beds and the continuing stiff competition for customers from resorts farther away from the southern end of Onondaga Lake.

Unique Attractions For Some Strange Groups

Like the other Onondaga Lake amusement parks, White City tried to increase attendance by encouraging a variety of groups to attend. During the first week after its opening, the management of White City invited 1,000 *Syracuse Journal* newsboys, free of charge, to experience the pleasures of the new resort. In connection with this promotion, the *Syracuse Journal* arranged for Eddie Watson, the "King of Newsboys of Kansas City," to come and talk to the boys about how to make a quick sale of the newspaper.

In 1907, news articles describe various outings and excursions to the park sponsored by local groups, such as employees of the Hunter Tupper store. That same season over one hundred members of the "Mystique Krewe" had an outing at White City, arriving in special trolley cars. In a July 20, 1906, article in the *Post Standard* it was reported, "the Krewe men wore their masks and dominos. Fred R. Peck, chairman of the entertainment committee, was the marshal, and he wore full Indian regalia. Chief J. M. Hull also had on his paint and feathers. . . . Two cars were filled with Indians and the drum corps played on the way to the White City while the members of the Krewe sang."[9] This oddly named group was part of the Letter Carriers Union, only one small group of businessmen and professionals in Syracuse who would sponsor a Ka-Noo-No Karnival each year in conjunction with State Fair Week to encourage visitors to stay in Syracuse.

The July 4 celebration at White City was an extravaganza that drew a large crowd. A live band played patriotic music and Mr. Minting, a unicyclist direct from the London Hippodrome, made a "daring ascent and descent of a mammoth spiral tower 75 feet high twice daily. The music program included a piece titled, "Recollections of the War." The production necessitates the use of eighteen cannons that fired by electricity from the bandstand."[10]

Grand Dancing Pavilion, "White City," Syracuse, N. Y.

3.10 Grand Dancing Pavilion, "White City," Syracuse, N.Y., postmarked 1907, message: "Well I say let's go to White city" on front of card, author's collection.

Roving vaudeville and circus acts were very popular at the beginning of the twentieth century. Vaudeville performances were usually comic, consisting of dialogue intermingled with light songs and dance. A regular singer at the concert facilities was Bert Morphy, popular for his loud baritone voice that would carry over the park. "Gertie Wood, a pretty little girl. . .who performs vocal gymnastics, and Sam J. Rasco who would sing Seabrook's Song of All Nations,"[11] were among the performers. Comedians of the time used slapstick humor and impersonated famous people from the past. Some of the circus acts included the likes of Mr. Dare Devil Dash, clad in red tights, who rode a bicycle down a ramp and would dive into the artificial lagoon to electrify the crowd of onlookers. "Dash says that the dive into the tank of water, which is practically ice-cold, is anything but a pleasant sensation these chilly June evenings. Long familiarity with the danger attached to the work has hardened him to it."[12]

3.11 Advertisement for "Dare Devil Dash," *Syracuse Journal*, June 4, 1907, page 13, Syracuse Public Library microfilm collection.

One of the more colorful tales associated with White City involved the demise of a pet donkey. The animal was part of one of the traveling circuses that frequented the amusement grounds in 1906. Its caretakers trained the donkey to feed from a bottle of beer, causing the poor beast to stagger about the grounds. "Pretty soon everyone knew of the donkey and why he acted as he did and paid no heed to the animal. One day the unfortunate creature, carrying his usual load of hop extract, stumbled in front of a moving (trolley) car and was killed. . . . More than one person grieved over the loss of the little burro."[13] Today such irresponsible treatment of an animal would earn a person jail time or a hefty fine for animal cruelty.

With the introduction of silent movies, J. L. Carolla and Fred Pellegrini, owners of the Grand Theater in Syracuse, were asked to run the Edison Theater at White City. One show, " 'Princess Lala, the Serpentine Dancer', starred Arthur McDonald singing, 'In the Valley Where the Bluebells Grow', with a lot of pictures to show the bluebells and the girl."[14]

In 1906, Onondaga Lake was still crystal clear in most places, and the creation of White City only twelve minutes from Clinton Square on the trolley line had seemed a sound investment to Mr. C. D. Beebe. Today the remains of White City lie under many feet of waste, with Route 690 passing over part of the amusement park. The longevity of this beautiful amusement park, inspired by the White City of the Columbian Exposition, lasted only three years as a popular attraction, far shorter than any other Onondaga Lake resort.

Notes

1. "C. D. Beebe Rural Trolley Pioneer Dies," *Syracuse Herald Journal* 19 February, 1939.

2. "Historic Onondaga Lake," Walter Schmidt, unpublished notes, 1985.

3. "Forty Thousand See White City," *Syracuse Post Standard* 31 May 1906.

4. "Forty Thousand See White City."

5. Denyse Clifford, "White City,"Onondaga Historical Association, 1985.

6. "White City to Open Tomorrow," *Syracuse Journal* 29 May 1906.

7. Advertisement, *Post Standard* 7 July 1908.

8. "Sketches of Yesterday, White City," A. J. Christopher, *The Jordan Leader* 23 November 1962.

9. "First Outing Had by Krewe," *Post Standard* 20 July 1907.

10. "Big Fourth Planned at White City," *Post Standard* 29 June 1907.

11. "White City Changes," Franklin H. Chase, 16 July 1907, cited by Denyse Clifford, archives of the Onondaga Historical Association.

12. "Skating Popular at White City," *Syracuse Post Standard* 12 June 1907.

13. "Sketches of Yesterday, White City," A. J. Christopher, *The Jordan Leader* 23 November 1962.

14. "White City Changes," Franklin H. Chase, 11 June 1907, cited by Denyse Clifford, archives of Onondaga Historical Association

Chapter 4
Added Attractions:
The Syracuse Yacht Club, 1898-1917,
The Onondaga Lake Marina,
and
The New York State Fair

Today commuters en route to work on Route 690 in Syracuse pass the fairgrounds exit, across from Crucible Steel, without realizing that at this spot the luxurious clubhouse of the Syracuse Yacht Club was once located. In August 1898, the first yacht club in Syracuse, the Syracuse Steam Yacht Club, was organized. The first yachts were steam-propelled, as this was before the advent of gasoline engine-powered boats. The fleet at the time consisted of twelve steam-powered boats.

The first meeting of this private boat club was held at the council chambers of the Syracuse City Hall, and a speech was given by the then mayor, James K. McGuire. Lyman C. Smith, the Syracuse typewriter king, was elected as the club's first president. It was decided that a clubhouse would be built on Onondaga Lake just south of Lake View Point. Rapid Transit Company had made an offer to have

4.1 View on Boulevard, Syracuse, N.Y., The Hugh C. Leighton Co. Mfgs. Portland, Maine, USA, printed in Frankfurt/Main, Germany, No. 2947, postmarked 1906, owned by author.

the clubhouse built on the southwest side of the harbor at Iron Pier. The railway people stressed, "The harbor was constructed at great expense and might well be utilized by the club."[1]

The clubhouse building was a massive wooden structure built on spikes driven into the lake bottom, at a cost of $30,000. At that time State Fair Boulevard was a hard-packed gravel road built upon fill between the lake and the trolley tracks. This turn-of-the twentieth-century postcard of State Fair Boulevard was taken looking northwest, showing the trolley line on the west side and Onondaga Lake on the east. The large size of the Syracuse Yacht Club can be appreciated even from a distance. The double decker open-air electric trolley is making a return trip from the resorts on the west shore of the lake. The writing on the top of this card, postmarked 1906, captures the moment: "Gee Whizz – How we did whiz along here." Imagine the thrill of riding on top of a double decker trolley at speeds much faster than most cars of this time.

This photo below was taken from the boulevard looking directly at the imposing clubhouse. The boulevard was built in 1893 on top of Solvay Process waste which was used to fill in the marshland around the southern portion of the lake. To the north of the two and a half story clubhouse were several boathouses that were imposing in their own right.

4.2 Yacht Club House, Onondaga Lake, Syracuse, N.Y., Onondaga Co. Parks, Office of Museums.

The newly constructed Syracuse Yacht Club quickly became one of the area's leading social centers, with a membership of 2,000. Daily luncheons and dinners were served. At its peak, 150 launches and sailboats were anchored at the club, and big racing events were scheduled during the various summer holidays. As time went on, steam-propelled yachts were replaced with tube boiler engines and then gasoline engines for speedboats. The boat *Echo* was built by Tom Milton of Brewerton, and was equipped with a twin gasoline motor. "The boat *Echo* had a speed of about

15 miles per hour. Enthusiasm grew rapidly–the steam yachts went [out] with the horse and buggy."[2]

This beautiful handpainted postcard of the Syracuse Yacht Club at sunset shows how immense the wooden structure was, built on pilings over Onondaga Lake. On the first story was a large dance floor and bar, with a wide veranda around much of the building. Nick Sarno of Solvay wistfully remembered being at the Yacht Club. "It was a pleasure to dance in the cool breezes blown in off the waters of the lake."[3] He frequented the establishment during the summer evenings. At various times during the summer, small sailboats were anchored around the clubhouse, and nearby boat-houses protected the boats from bad weather and provided storage during the winter.

4.3 Yacht Club House, Onondaga Lake, Syracuse, N.Y., The Rotograph Co., New York City and Germany, No. G7173, no postmark, author's collection.

4.4 The Syracuse University crew in front of Yacht Club, turn of the twentieth century, Onondaga Yacht Club.

The Yacht Club was instrumental in forming and fostering the Syracuse University rowing crews that were and continue to be housed on the Onondaga Lake Outlet, across from Long Branch Park. For many years, the National Rowing Regattas were held on Onondaga Lake, and to this day Syracuse University and Liverpool High School crews can be seen training for future meets in the Onondaga Lake outlet. This old postcard shows the Syracuse University crew facilities at the beginning of the twentieth century.

4.5 Syracuse University crew facilities at Onondaga Lake outlet to Seneca River, not dated. Onondaga Co. Parks, Office of Museums.

During the long winter months, club members often returned to the clubhouse to take part in iceboat racing, replacing yachting as a popular weekend pastime. The speed at which these crafts could go was exhilarating, but one had to be careful about coming onto open water caused by ice harvesting, thaws, or being too close to running water from various tributaries to Onondaga Lake.

The Syracuse Yacht Club's building came to a rather premature end on May 10, 1917, when fire broke out, destroying the clubhouse and several boats nearby. When the fire was discovered at 2:25 AM, the proprietor G. L. Bartoo ran around making sure the boarders evacuated quickly, and by 3:00 AM nothing was left but burning pilings. In the years just before the fire, the old Yacht Club had been used as a boarding house for workers at the nearby steel works. With the coming of motorboats and the automobile, interest in yachting began to wane. The surviving boathouses would eventually be doomed by the unsightly waste beds of the Solvay Process Company that were expanding along the southwestern shoreline. After the fire, "activity shifted to the present Onondaga Yacht Club near Liverpool, where we will see some fast going [boats]–70 miles per hour plus."[4]

Building a New Marina on the East Shore

As the west shore of Onondaga Lake began a long period of decline from the turn-of-the-century through the early 1930s, the east shore was being developed, thanks to the Great Depression. One of the first work relief programs in the

United States was the Onondaga County Emergency Work Bureau which put over two thousand men to work building Onondaga County Park between 1931 and 1933. The abandoned Oswego Canal was filled in as well as the extensive swampland, and in its place picnic areas were built, along with the Salt Museum, the Ste. Marie Jesuit Mission, and Danforth Salt Lake on top of the old salt springs. Also, the old Mud Lock was restored for future generations.

It was not until 1935 that work crews built the Onondaga Lake Marina, within the newly established park on the east shore. This is the nearest harbor to Syracuse for private craft traveling to Central New York by way of the Barge Canal that helps link the St. Lawrence River to the Mississippi River. Vessels ranging from large cruisers to outboards and sailboats may dock at the marina from May 15 to November 15. Slips at the marina can be rented by the month or season with electricity available along the front wall.

4.6 Photograph of Onondaga Lake Marina, Liverpool, 1941, Onondaga Co. Parks, Office of Museums.

This 1941 photograph shows a boat entering the Onondaga Marina Harbor with larger boats in slips along the east wall. On the lower right corner of this picture can be seen three seaplanes along the shoreline. Originally, plans called for a seaplane base, as shown in this 1940 plan for the Yacht Harbor in Liverpool. Today the seaplane base has been abandoned, but floating docks have been placed inside the harbor to better accommodate more pleasure boats.

On October 11, 1940, First Lady Eleanor Roosevelt arrived by seaplane at the Port Onondaga Sea Plane Base. In this picture, she is being greeted on the floating dock by local officials and photographers. Later that day she was taken to the Salt Museum and other sites on the east shore of Onondaga Lake Park to see what

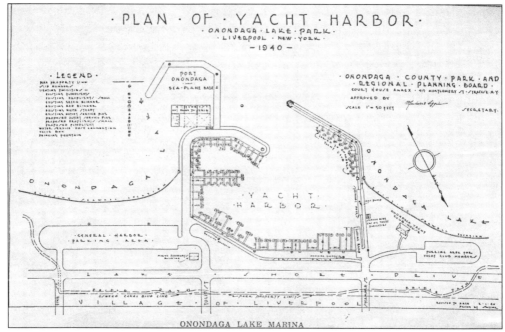

4.7 Plan of Yacht Harbor, Onondaga Lake Park, Liverpool, 1940, Onondaga County Park and Regional Planning Board, Onondaga Co. Parks, Office of Museums.

had been started during the emergency work relief programs while her husband was still the governor of New York State. After her one-day visit to Onondaga County, she again boarded the seaplane at Onondaga Yacht Basin for her return flight to Poughkeepsie.

During the late-nineteenth century, Central New York had two yacht clubs, the Syracuse Steam Yacht Club previously discussed, and the Onondaga Yacht Club.

4.8 Eleanor Roosevelt on seaplane dock, October 11, 1940, photo by Herbert Cate, Onondaga Co. Parks, Office of Museums.

Based upon the map that was part of the June 20, 1887, Opening Regatta on Onondaga Lake, the Onondaga Yacht Club was located in the vicinity of Ley Creek in the southeastern corner of the lake. The Onondaga Yacht Club's members followed a challenging sailboat course from Lake View Point to Liverpool, down the lake to the Blast Furnace (now Crucible Steel), and returning to the finish line off Lake View Point. Five sailboats entered the race that day to compete for the top prize of sixteen dollars.

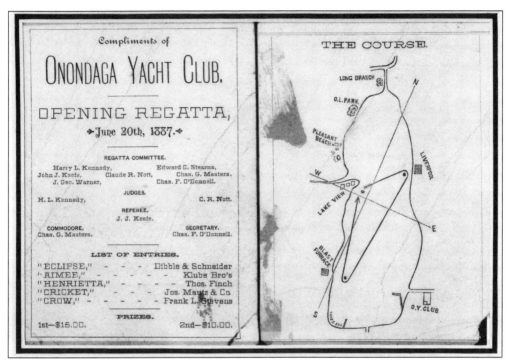

4.9 Onondaga Yacht Club regatta program, June 20, 1887, Onondaga Yacht Club archives.

The Onondaga Yacht Club building can be viewed in the picture of the Onondaga Lake Marina, just to the north of the yacht harbor. The following picture of the Yacht Club building was taken during the 1950s and shows the three additions made to the building, which originally was constructed in 1938. The Onondaga Yacht Club is within the Onondaga Lake Park and leases the land from the county.

The current Onondaga Yacht Club was started by Max Wagner and a group of boaters who had met for several years in private homes, at the Syracuse Hotel, and at Heids in Liverpool. The current structure was built in 1938 and was added to at least three times. Even before the clubhouse was built, the Onondaga Yacht Club sponsored a speedboat championship regatta sanctioned by the American Power Boat Association on May 29 and 30, 1937. In this newspaper announcement on May 27, 1937, the club declared that the race was dedicated to the completion of the Onondaga Lake Park Yacht Harbor and that their race headquarters was at the Heid's Hotel. The racecourse was one and a quarter mile with boats in a variety of classes circling the course four times, for a total of five miles.

4.10 Photograph of Onondaga Yacht Club, 1950s, archives of Onondaga Yacht Club.

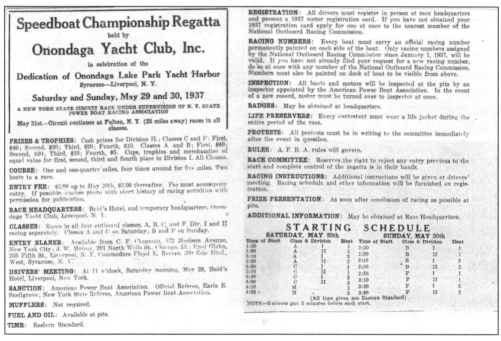

4.11 Announcement of speedboat championship regatta, May 29, and 30, 1937, *Syracuse Herald Journal*, **May 27, 1937, archives of Onondaga Yacht Club.**

The original structure for the Yacht Club was completed in 1938 with workers from the Works Progress Administration doing the work of painting it. By this time, Franklin D. Roosevelt was president of the United States and was using some of the same methods nationwide that were used successfully locally in the early 1930s to build the Onondaga Lake Park. This picture shows unemployed men painting the clubhouse while the commodore and other club members look on. The caption at the top of this picture reads, "slow-men-at work," probably a derogatory comment on how slow these unemployed workers got the job done.

4.12 W.P.A. painting bee of OYA, June 24, 1938, archives of Onondaga Yacht Club.

In an interview with Gary Klink, the current Onondaga Yacht Club historian, he said that the 1937 race was the only powerboat race that the club sponsored, but that there have been many powerboat races on Onondaga Lake up to the present time. The current Onondaga Yacht Club was established in 1934 to promote the use of Onondaga Lake for boating, and since the 1930s, they have marked hazardous obstacles around the lake and have sponsored numerous sailboat races. In 1948, the club sponsored the Syracuse Centennial Regatta at which Governor Thomas Dewey was in attendance. In 1981, the club sponsored the Eastern Regional National Sports Festival, where surfboard sailboaters were picked for the U.S. Olympic Team. The Onondaga Yacht Club still holds an annual invitational regatta open to all classes of sailboats. But membership in the Yacht Club is down from the peak years of the early 1960s. Up until the late 1950s, the Onondaga Yacht Club sponsored iceboat races, a wintertime tradition that goes back to the golden age of the west shore lake resorts.

Today, historian Gary Klink observes that Onondaga Lake has come a long way since the peak pollution years of the 1950s. "Once oil barges added to the lake pollution from oil spills at the barge canal terminal, but today different types of fish are increasing and there are not just carp to be seen. Zebra mussels now cling to the dock pilings, but they are helping to filter the polluted waters of Onondaga Lake."[5]

The New York State Fair, 1890-2000

The New York State Fair has been held across State Fair Boulevard opposite Lake View Point since 1890. This late summer tradition was not always located on Onondaga Lake's west shore. When the New York State Agricultural Society established a fair to promote agriculture, it was held near the old county courthouse in Syracuse on September 29, and 30, 1841. The site was located between the rival villages of Syracuse and Salina at North Salina and Division Street.

The State Fair then moved to a variety of New York State cities for the next forty-eight years, returning once in 1849 to Syracuse, when the fair was held on the James Street Hill site on the city's northeast side. Vice President Millard Fillmore and Senator Henry Clay from Kentucky gave speeches; two prizefighters gave a series of exhibition bouts, but an early model of a Ferris wheel, "served as a beacon to the 65,000 visitors who traveled (to the fair). The structure was a great iron and oaken wheel with wooden bucket cars, large enough to carry either four adults or six children aloft from the end of each of the four arms."[6] Fifty years later, G. W. Gale Ferris created the giant steam-powered Ferris wheel for the 1893 World's Columbian Exhibition in Chicago. The Exhibition claimed this Ferris Wheel to be an original invention, ignoring its earlier advent at the 1849 New York State Fair.

4.13 Sketch of 1849 New York State Fair at Syracuse, author's collection.

In 1887, James Geddes was elected president of the State Agricultural Society and campaigned to have the permanent location of the fair in Syracuse. In 1889, a 100-acre tract of pasture land was purchased for $30,000, "adjacent to both the tracks of the New York Central and the Erie Canal, yet within easy access to the city's business district."[7] That same year, livestock buildings and a half-mile race-track were built on this site; the last of the traveling state fairs was held in Albany that September.

The main entrance to the fair was built across the road from what remained of the Powell Stock Farm. This 1900 postcard illustrates the fashions of the day, with some walking to the train terminal and others driving cars through the entrance gate.

4.14 Main entrance to New York State Fair, 1900, no postmark, author's collection.

September 11, 1890 was the opening day of the permanent New York State Fair at Syracuse. It poured all day and half way through the second day of the fair. Still, thousands attended to see a huge tank full of game fish in the horticulture hall, "and a family tree made of human hair from more than 150 persons—all for 50 cents."[8] An enterprising commercial fisherman named Mr. Andrewson obtained a beached whale from the New Jersey coast, and immersed it in sixty barrels of embalming fluid, thus developing a "whale of a show" that he took by barge down the waterways of the Northeast, arriving in Syracuse on the Erie Canal just in time for the fair. In spite of its odor, this marine curiosity was a booming financial success, even though the first fair itself was not.

Like today, food was a major attraction from the start at the State Fair. While thrifty farm wives often arrived with their wagons laden with homemade bounty, more exotic fare enticed fairgoers: oysters, new-fangled frankfurters, exotic fruits such as bananas, nuts, candy, popcorn, sausages, and a local Syracuse invention, the salt potato. Even in the early days of the State Fair entrepreneurs opened booths to sell merchandise such as china, glassware, and jewelry.

As with the State Fair today, everything from produce and flowers to various types of animals were judged. One amusing anecdote from around the turn of the twentieth century involved a woman who was inspecting a rooster exhibit. As she leaned towards the cage for a closer look, the rooster snatched one of her diamond earrings. Upon hearing the lady's screams, the owner of the bird rushed over but refused to decapitate his award-winning rooster to retrieve the stone from its gullet. He did, however, come up with a novel and satisfactory solution; "he just bought the other stone too, and fed it to the bird the following noon before an appreciative crowd attracted by appropriate advertising."[9]

Another tale of State Fair skull duggery centered around the apple-judging contest. The judge was about to award first place to a display of perfectly beautiful Baldwin and Russet apples. "The judge noticed a slight depression under the sticker used to label the variety. On checking further, he found the sticker covered a hole and that someone was at home [inside]."[10] This entry was immediately disqualified, as were the other entries by the same apple grower, who attempted to disguise his wormy apples several times.

In succeeding years, crowds were enticed by large Japanese fireworks displays and trotting and chariot races at the half-mile racetrack. The DL&W Railroad made the journey convenient and affordable by having their trains leave Syracuse every half hour, "with fares 10 cents one way and 15 cents round trip."[11]

During the Gay Nineties the State Fair was rustic with many exhibits in tents, dirt roads, and a few wooden sidewalks serving as the means to get around. When bicycling became a popular fad, in the 1890s, bicycle races were held with the winners receiving a diamond stud as a prize. The midway of the fair was constantly expanding each year, and its popularity then rivaled that of today. At the 1895 State Fair, during the golden age of the lake's west shore, the midway included the following features: "the Blarney Castle, the Palace of Illusions, the Persian Theater, and Cairo Street."[12] The following postcard, postmarked 1911, shows a Wild West entertainment on the right, and the smoke stacks of the Solvay Process Company can be seen off in the distance. The only message on the back of the card reads, "Weather fine, and plenty of racing," which shows the sender's favorite leisure activity.

4.15 General view of midway, Syracuse fair, published by Ralph Finney, Times Square Station, New York City, postmarked 1911, author's collection.

In 1900, the state took over management of the fair from the Agricultural Society to make costly improvements to the fairgrounds. That same year the state legislature provided funds to build a mile track to lure the nation's top racing attractions that would in turn increase revenue from people betting on horses. Many of the large buildings still in use today were built on the fairgrounds shortly after the state took over financial control of the fair.

The postcard that follows, postmarked 1906, shows hundreds viewing a parade in downtown Syracuse. For about ten years, the idea of establishing an annual nighttime carnival to coincide with the State Fair was initiated by the Chamber of Commerce. During the early years of the State Fair, there were no live performances to entertain fairgoers at night, unlike today where evening shows by big-name performers draw large crowds. "Patterned after New Orleans's Mardi Gras, but without the pre-Lenten significance, the Syracuse project was called the Kanoona Karnival, a combination of Indian lore, history and community fun, all under bright electrical displays in downtown streets."[13] *Kanoono* was believed to be of Mohawk derivation, meaning a well-watered land to which Syracuse is well suited with two canals and nearby Onondaga Lake.

4.16 A street scene during State Fair, postmarked 1906, no publisher listed, author's collection.

The Ka-Noo-No Karnival was organized in 1905 to attract visitors to the State Fair, encouraging them to stay overnight in Syracuse, and quickly became known as "the Mardi Gras of the North." This weeklong event was free of charge to the public, as it was sponsored by the business and professional community with the realization that the visitors would boost the local economy, much as sporting events are vied for by cities today. During State Fair week, concerts were held at Clinton Square, with special events each night. A float parade representing mythological subjects and a 'grand water pageant spectacle' was held on the Erie Canal on Wednesday, and a special school children's parade was held on Friday, with all of the city schools represented. Illustration 4.17 shows the passing of the water pageant in front of the Soldiers and Sailors Monument in Clinton Square. Lights from the Electric Railway Station can be seen in the distance, where visitors and natives alike would get the trolley for the State Fair and west shore resorts.

4.17 Grand water pageant on Erie Canal, Ka-Noo-No Karnival program, Syracuse, Sept. 11-16, 1911, author's collecction.

4.18 School children's parade, Ka-Noo-No Karnival program, Syracuse, Sept. 11-16, 1911, author's collcction.

Illustration 4.18 shows one of the city schools parading at night past thousands of people lining the streets of Syracuse. Each school had its own theme, such as the Seasons, Ireland, Pied Piper of Hamlin, Ye Olden Times, and many others.

The 1903 State Fair was special for several reasons. President Theodore Roosevelt attended the fair, giving a fifty-eight-minute speech before a crowd of 15,000, watched closely by secret service men, so soon after the assassination of President McKinley. The Women's Building was opened and the upstart automobiles made their first race at the mile track. Special trains carried passengers on the New York Central and Lackawanna lines, and it was said that the Lakeside trolleys carried up to forty thousand to the fair in one day.

In 1905, Carl E. Meyers, drew large crowds as he navigated his airship, containing 7,000 cubic feet of gas, between the State Fair's large buildings. In 1910, De Lloyd Thompson, the king of aviators, flew his biplane over the infield of the racetrack, demonstrating precision bombing and a loop-the-loop. At one point his motor stopped and the plane dropped fifty feet from the ground before pulling out of the dive. This old postcard shows two biplanes flying over the racetrack as thousands of spectators view the thrills from the grandstand.

Flying Airships at New York State Fair, Syracuse, N. Y.

4.19 "Flying Airships" (biplanes) at New York State Fair, Syracuse, N.Y., published by Ralph Finney, N.Y., no postmark, author's collection.

In April 1917, the United States entered World War I, and the State Fair grounds became a major installation known as Camp Syracuse. In the spring, some ten thousand horses were assembled for service with field artillery, ambulances, and ammunition trains, and later during the summer, seventeen thousand soldiers were trained at Camp Syracuse. Cattle, livestock, and horticulture buildings became barracks, and tents were put up under the grandstand and throughout much of the fairgrounds. On September 10, 1917, the State Fair opened as usual, with the war and production of food products as major themes. "Each day there were military drills, trench warfare in sham battles, barbed wire entanglement problems and other military demonstrations."[14]

Camp Syracuse closed down on November 1, because of the harsh Central New York winter climate, but reopened in 1918 to train eleven thousand limited service troops, not destined for front line service. "Arrivals at the fair were greeted by a tremendous victory arch, rising 20 feet above the main entrance, with a span of 60 feet. It was dedicated to the men of the state who had already given their lives."[15]

The State Fair has been an annual event at Syracuse since 1890, except for six years during the 1940s. Restaurants were first set up under tents by local churches to raise money. The fairgrounds now cover approximately 360 acres and have parking lots to accommodate over thirty-five thousand cars. Fairgoers no longer come by train to the front gate, but many of the large buildings built almost one hundred years ago still are standing. This old postcard shows the 'Dairy and Grange Buildings' with cars parked in front of the large white columns, as military vehicles were later parked for fairgoers.

4.20 Dairy and grange buildings, N.Y. State Fair Grounds, Syracuse, N.Y., no postmark, author's collection.

The State Fair is now open to the public for ten days instead of the original two-day stand in 1890. The fairgrounds today are in use year-round, being used by over 220 outside activities besides the fair. Attendance records continue to be set as fairgoers continue to be drawn to the fourteen thousand-seat grandstand built in 1975 for a wide variety of entertainment. Today, the New York State Fairgrounds is the only holdover from the golden age of lakeside resorts on the west shore of Onondaga Lake, as all of the resort buildings have been torn down.

Notes

1. "Yacht Club Declines," *Syracuse Post Standard* 17 June 1899.

2. L. G. Van Wagner, "Onondaga Lake a Mecca for Sports," Letter to the Editor, *Syracuse Post Standard* 18 August 1948.

3. Joe Ganley, Feature Column, *Syracuse Herald Journal* 20 November 1979.

4. L. G. Van Wagner, "Onondaga Lake a Mecca for Sports," Letter to the Editor, *Syracuse Post Standard* 18 August 1948.

5. Personal interview with Gary Klink, historian of Onondaga Yacht Club, May 2000.

6. Henry Schramm, *Empire Showcase, A History of the NY State Fair*, North Country Books, Inc., 1985.

7. Henry Schramm, *Empire Showcase.*

8. Henry Schramm, *Empire Showcase.*

9. Henry Schramm, *Empire Showcase.*

10. Henry Schramm, *Empire Showcase.*

11. Henry Schramm, *Empire Showcase.*

12. Walter H. Schmidt, "Historic Onondaga Lake, The New York State Fair," unpublished notes, 1988.

13. Henry Schramm, *Empire Showcase.*

14. Henry Schramm, *Empire Showcase.*

15. Henry Schramm, *Empire Showcase.*

CHAPTER 5
LAKE VIEW POINT RESORT,
ONONDAGA LAKE'S EARLIEST RESORT,
1872-1915

Lake View Point was formed by thousands of years of silt built up at the mouth of Nine Mile Creek, washed from the highlands of Marcellus, all the way back to Otisco Lake. Because of its spectacular vantage point on Onondaga Lake, after the Civil War, Lake View Point became the scene of chowder parties, similar to today's clambakes. From this promontory, one can see the city of Syracuse against the mountains to the south, the village of Liverpool on the east shore, and Maple Bay to the north. In 1872, Fred Ganier of Liverpool decided to start the first vacation retreat on Onondaga Lake. At that time, the delta formed by Nine Mile Creek was forested by lofty elm trees, and the point was also known as Deer Point because deer often came out of the brush and into the open here.

This spot, with its panoramic view and cool breezes, was an ideal place to while away hot summer afternoons, and it became the first recreational spot on the lake. However, it was also one of the first to vanish into history. Because the delta was low, the grounds often were flooded, especially during the spring, limiting the growth potential of Lake View Point compared to other resort sites on the lake. The Point was in close proximity to Solvay Process Company, and, in time, the delta was used to dump chemical waste to such an extent that the point is now completely covered with refuse. Nine Mile Creek's water is presently an unhealthy-looking yellow due to the continual leaching of the waste beds.

Early Development of Lake View Point

During the summer of 1871, Captain Fred Ganier provided temporary accommodations and ran a little steamer to introduce many Syracusans to the beautiful scenery of Lake View Point. During the following winter he began improvements, using a pile driver to erect a pier and landing for his future passengers' convenience. "An ice-house has been constructed and filled with sixty tons of lake ice, ready for the summer excursionists. The grove has been cleared of undergrowth . . . . A house of two stories, 32 x 34 feet is now in process of construction, to be placed in a position on the little bay commanding a beautiful view."[1] This is the picture of the Lake View Hotel that Fred Ganier had built in 1872.

By July 20, 1872, the steamer *Sperry* began running regularly at 10:00 AM from the packet boat dock at Clinton Square, returning in the evening, for fifty cents

5.1 The Lake View Hotel, date unknown, Onondaga Co. Parks Office of Museums.

round-trip. "The *Sperry* will also run between Fred Ganier's dock at Salina and Geddes and Lake View Point every ninety minutes during the day. Fare twenty-five cents."[2] The advertisement that follows, from the July 3, 1872 *Syracuse Standard*, stresses the central location of Lake View Point only three miles up Onondaga Lake.

SUMMER RESORTS.

LAKE VIEW POINT!

GREAT SPECIALITIES!

To the Citizens of Syracuse and Vicinity:

A DELIGHTFUL RESORT !

Come and See ! You Will Find it So !

The most central, easily reached, and every way the Most attractive place in Central New York. It is Pleasantly located, about three miles up the Onondaga Lake. The cheapest place to go, and the most easily Place for public and private parties to go out of the city.
⇨ Parties can go and return any hour of day by Steamboat. Steamboat touching at Geddes, Salina, and Liverpool, every hour of the day.
FRED GANIER, Proprietor

5.2 Summer resorts advertisement for Lake View Point, July 3, 1872, *Syracuse Standard*, Syracuse Public Library microfilm collection.

During the 1870s, the popularity of chowder parties at Lake View Point continued, with patrons arriving at the point by steamer or carriage. One article in the *Syracuse Journal* of August 1873 said that the Onondaga Lake Club members came with their wives, children, and friends for a basket picnic. Nothing marred the enjoyment of the group as they, "happily spent [it] in singing, dancing, croquet-playing and lunching. The party returned home by way of the Oswego Canal, reaching the packet basin at precisely ten minutes of ten last night."[3] Besides these weekend excursions to the Point for chowder parties and picnics, at least once there was a memorial excursion to commemorate the landing of the French Jesuit Fathers at the Point on September 5, 1654. Fred Ganier had several prominent speakers give addresses, followed by entertainment.

FOR SALE.

A RARE CHANCE! – Owing to my being troubled
With rheumatism all spring

I WILL OFFER FOR SALE

LAKE VIEW!

OR ONE INDIVIDUAL HALF !

Lake View is one of the finest and best located place in Central
New York, being located half way up the lake, overlooks
Syracuse, Liverpool and all the lake, is well shaded, and
is the best located place in these parts for Picnic, Private
Parties, and Moonlight Excursions. The lake is getting
very popular, having four splendid steamboats on the lake.

LAKE VIEW

Will be open to the public, July 1, 1874.
FRED GANIER, Proprietor,
17 Wolf Street, Syracuse.

5.3 For Sale advertisement for Lake View, *Syracuse Standard,* July 1, 1874, Syracuse Public Library microfilm collection.

As Fred Ganier was busy making Lake View Point a favorite stop for excursions, he had difficulties from time to time. In 1874, he was ready to sell his popular resort because of his increasingly painful rheumatism. During the mid-1880s, Owen Donovan sold his lease of Lake View because of a conflict with Mr. Ganier.

During the decade of the 1870s, not everyone enthusiastically supported the social activities going on at Lake View and other budding resorts on Onondaga Lake. At the end of the decade, on March 14, 1879, the *Syracuse Journal* mentioned a growing movement for the suppression of boisterous parties on Sundays at the picnic groves along the shores of Onondaga Lake. Later that year, the *Syracuse Courier* reported that as many as six thousand left for Lake View Point and other spots with, "the hegira beginning before the church bells tolled the worshiper to their devotions, and continued till nightfall. The most popular route was via Geddes [Pier], the railway company having a line to that point, having provided conveyance, to the water's edge, from the city at a very trifling expense. Two steamboats plied up and down the lake all day long, being loaded too heavily for safety on nearly every trip. Lake View Point commanded the greatest popularity."[4]

About twenty years later, in 1899, the *Syracuse Herald* was still reporting on the displeasure expressed by area houses of worship concerning Onondaga Lake resorts having gambling machines available to the public on Sundays. "Sunday, as a day of rest and quiet, isn't down on the resort keeper's calendar. Everything is run on Sunday as it is on any other day. The 'Coney Island man' is open, and so are the theaters. It is the so-called 'Continental Sabbath' exemplified. Baseball, about which the Ministerial Association raised such a fuss in Syracuse, is played on Sunday, and it is one of the most innocent of the amusements."[5] Today, church restrictions on what is considered appropriate behavior on Sunday have been largely relaxed to the extent that services are even offered on Saturday night to free up modern leisure seekers so they can find enjoyment to their hearts' content on a Sunday.

During the early 1880s, Lake View Point seemed to be very popular, competing with Cowan's Grove (Pleasant Beach) and Long Branch for the favorite weekend picnic spot. One article in 1880 referred to Lake View Point as the Coney Island of Syracuse, with steamers making hourly trips from Geddes and Salina Piers. The June 27, 1881, *Syracuse Courier* reported that, "Lake View had the usual number of Sunday visitors, but Cowan's Grove and Long Branch were comparatively dull. The weather was all that could be desired with not a ripple on the water."[6]

What was it like to go for an outing at Lake View Point in the 1880s? Most people would take the North Salina streetcar to the Salina Pier. The streetcar would be crowded with men and women of every age and description. The women typically would wear light-colored summer dresses, embellished with decorative ribbons. The crowds would be in good humor and did not complain of the summer heat. At the last stop on the line the crowd would get off and walk, "over the central freight tracks and down the wide path of sand and gravel leading to the [Salina] pier, a sixteenth of a mile distant."[7] Two steamers stopped at Salina Pier about half an hour apart, and would leave for Lake View Point filled to capacity. Round-trip tickets on the steamer cost thirty-five cents. Once at Lake View Point, the steamer discharged hundreds of passengers while a band heralded this arrival. Most disembarked here, but a few continued the journey to Cowan's Grove or to Long Branch. The Lake View bar did a thriving business, and so did the shooting gallery by its side. "The young men and maidens wandered far out into the woods."[8] The band was stationed under the tall trees, with entertainment provided by local groups like the Otis Brass and String Band. Because the old dancing platform was in a dilapidated state, those inclined to dance, resorted to the turf. Sometimes entertainment at the Point featured exciting boxing exhibitions.

Harmony Did Not Always Prevail at the Point

Not everything was harmonious with the huge groups that frequented Lake View Point. The large crowds would mill around for hours, and lager beer flowed freely from the tap until 5:00 in the afternoon. Sometimes the decorum of large picnic groups of five thousand people would be shattered by gangs of 'roughs' that possibly had had too much lager during the afternoon. On one of the return trips of the steamer *Jacob Amos* two young men from a Concordia picnic got into a fight. They "commenced to pummel each other to the terror of a crowd of ladies on the boat. A young man, bartender for Thomas Abele, attempted to quiet the disputants and had the end of his finger bitten off. The fighting continued after the boat reached the pier at Salina and both young men retired from sheer exhaustion from the contest with bloody noses, blackened eyes and swollen heads."[9]

Another time at a Coopers' Union picnic at Lake View Point, a young man named Butts and two lady companions were assaulted, while on a walk to gather wildflowers. Two roughs knocked Butts down and assaulted the girls. Mr. Butts and one of the girls got back on their feet and fled the scene, leaving a Miss Josie Deis to the mercy of the two roughs. "Officer Shug was notified of the occurrence at a later hour last night, but at once set to work to find the villains, the only clue he had being the description given of them by Miss Deis."[10] Officer Shug arrested the two roughs in the early morning hours and Dr. Kempter was called in to examine the condition of Miss Deis. He reported that, "she has been brutally violated, and is in a very precarious state."[11]

Finding It Hard to Compete

By the end of the nineteenth century, Lake View Point was accessible by State Fair Boulevard (Van Vleck Road), steamboat, or train. The DL&W Railroad had eight passenger runs each day on the west shore of Onondaga Lake, all of which could have stopped at Lake View Point. There was a dirt road that extended away from the Point to connect the nearby boulevard and railroad. Lake View Point probably had its heyday during the 1890s, when Syracusans escaped the city on weekends to frequent the entertainment concessions such as a shooting gallery and a casino. The concessions never were as elaborate as the ones later developed by competing resorts on the west shore of the lake. During this same time period, the Solvay Process Company, which was established in 1884 to make soda ash from limestone and salt, began having increasing problems with disposal of its waste byproducts. This need for the expansion of the unsightly and, ultimately, polluting wastebeds put the nearby area resorts in jeopardy.

During the winter months, people continued to come to Lake View Point for iceboating, skating, and ice fishing. The resort saloon was kept open to provide refreshment to those that braved the winter weather. Once spring came, the Point became a jumping off point for fishermen. "Onondaga Lake was an angler's paradise then, the prize being a much-desired specie of white fish. . . . A boat livery catered to the nimrod's needs,"[12] providing rental boats to the many fishermen who arrived by train, boat, or highway.

In 1899, Frank Heberle, the last surviving son of the founder of Heberle Brewery, bought Lake View Point with plans to turn it into a private family resort, without the rowdy and drunken gangs that had clouded the resort's reputation. But he never was able to realize his dream, because by then the Solvay Process waste dumps had encroached too close to Lake View Point. Mr. Heberle's death in 1916 closed the park forever, and during that same year Syracuse began proceedings to acquire the thirty-seven acres of resort, with the intention of locating a sewage disposal plant there. When city plans for the site changed, they attempted to abandon the proceedings, but the Heberle estate held them to the agreement, eventually receiving $13,500 from the city in 1919.

As the new owners of the Point, the city of Syracuse made an agreement with the Solvay Process Company, "whereby the city was to have the privilege of mixing the sludge from its sewage plant with the lime waste being deposited on the shores of Onondaga Lake, while the company was to be allowed to use Lake View Point for a dumping ground for its waste by another contract made in 1925."[13] The dumping went on for decades on Lake View Point and the marshes along the southwestern shore of the lake. As this blight of the landscape continued on the west shore, "the Golden Age of the Onondaga Lake Resorts" receded into the past.

Many Plans to Preserve the Lakeshore of Onondaga Lake

As far back as 1847, Syracuse's first mayor, Harvey Baldwin, envisioned the preservation of the natural beauty surrounding Onondaga Lake for future generations. It was not until 1928 that a plan for a park around Onondaga Lake was proposed by the Onondaga Park and Regional Planning Board, a long time dream of its secretary, Joseph Griffin. Plans called for an airport and aviation school just south of Lake View Point, and the creation of a city park on the south shore.

As the Great Depression took hold of the country after 1929, New York enacted the Emergency Relief Act of September 1931. As a result of the passage of this act, the Onondaga County Work Relief Bureau was established by action of the County Board of Supervisors, eventually employing over two thousand people under the leadership of Crandall Melvin. These workers developed a county park along the east shore of Onondaga Lake on land abandoned by the Oswego Canal. The original plan for a trail around the lake was not achieved, but on the east shore a Salt Museum, the Ste. Marie French Mission to the Iroquois, and the reconstructed Mud Lock on the Oswego Canal were built. The success of the Onondaga County Work Relief Bureau served as a model for President Franklin D. Roosevelt's W.P.A., designed to provide jobs for Americans building parks and other public improvements throughout the country.

Plans for beautification of the west shore of Onondaga Lake were renewed in 1938 when the Civil Development Committee of One Hundred proposed plans that included a bathing beach, a hydroplane base, a riding and hunt club, a canoe and boat club, and an airport. Nothing came of this plan until the 1943 Thanksgiving Day break in a Solvay Process Company dike inundated a two-mile area of the fair grounds and State Fair Boulevard. People living in parts of the Lakeland area awoke at 3:00 AM on November 25, by what they thought was a storm. The *Syracuse Post Standard* reported that Mrs. George Pinkowski, "arose and went downstairs to find the waste lime oozing up through the heating register and covering the floors of the lower rooms. . . . The cellar was filled with the flood sludge that covered the furnace and the house grew cold quickly."[14] The chalky waste material was five feet deep in some places, and the initial wave carried parked cars at least one thousand feet, as well as sweeping away the Indian Village on the fair grounds. The picture that follows shows the full extent of the damage around Susco's Garage in Lakeland.

5.4 Susco's Garage in Lakeland during 1943 Solvay Process sludge spill. Margaret Valerino collection, *Syracuse Post Standard*, **November 26, 1943.**

Rescuers worked through Thanksgiving Day using bulldozers and boats to save humans and animals. Luckily, all were saved. The newspaper article went on to report that, "hundreds of Thanksgiving turkeys were eaten cold because entire families drove to the scene only to be turned back before they could get much of a view of the flooded section."[15] At least twenty rescuers had to be treated for chemical burns, which they suffered on the hands and legs, during their rescue efforts. The magnitude of the 1943 spill made a lot of people think about the loss of the lake's beauty. Two organizations, the Lakeland Taxpayers Association and the Onondaga Lake Reclamation Association pressed the state to take action against Solvay Process/Allied Chemical Company.

During the election of 1946, Governor Thomas Dewey seemed to be ready to take action against Solvay Process/Allied Chemical when he described Allied's pollution of Onondaga Lake as "the perfect outrage." [16] In 1948, Governor Dewey flew over Onondaga Lake and called Lake View Point, site of the Solvay Process/Allied Chemical dumping, a "man-made desert."[17] The 1938 aerial photo of Onondaga Lake clearly illustrates the total lack of vegetation on Lake View Point, in sharp contrast with the forested areas and fields that encircle the rest of the lake.

5.5 Aerial view of Onondaga Lake, 1938, Syracuse University Bird Library collection.

After the election, the governor did not follow through with promises to improve the quality of Onondaga Lake, and it was not until 1953 when Allied Chemical, to end the state procedures against the company resulting from the sludge spill, gave the state 400 acres of land to use for a State Fair parking lot, a five and a half mile expressway linking the State Thruway and Syracuse, and the recreational development of the west shore. Recreational development called for the eighty-foot-high barren mounds of alkali to be turned into an aquatic stadium, a golf course, a waterfront restaurant, and a bike trail, which would encircle the entire lake. The State Fair parking lot and Route 690 were built, but nothing came of the beautification projects to this day.

Today, Lake View Point still has up to eighty feet of waste, mostly calcium carbonate, on top of its once swampy shoreline that was once upon a time Onondaga Lake's first resort. During the 1940s, the prevailing thought was that nothing would grow on this man-made desert because the chalky white material lacked any organic materials such as phosphates. During the late 1960s, SUNY-Environmental Science and Forestry professor Norman Richards changed the landscape of Lake View Point by bringing in bags of fertilizer to make it possible for plants, shrubs, and trees to thrive in what was a perfect growing environment of good drainage and moisture. Now, at the turn of the twenty-first century, the Point supports a lush growth of trees and plants and has reverted back to the natural state that existed in the mid-1800s, when the spot was called Deer Point. This picture was taken on top of the waste beds looking out through the thick vegetation that now grows on Lake View Point. The Liverpool water tower can be seen across Onondaga Lake.

5.6 View of Lake View Point at turn of twenty-first century, photo by author, summer 2000.

In conclusion, Lake View Point was Onondaga Lake's first major resort in 1872, but its popularity was short-lived because of its low terrain and its unfortunate proximity to Solvay Process. Gradually, other amusement spots on the west shore with bigger and better attractions eclipsed Lake View Point's popularity, and as previously pointed out, the encroachment of the Solvay Process waste beds further hastened its demise.

5.7 View of soda ash waste embankment on Lake View Point, photo by author.

Notes

1. "Onondaga Lake, Its Beauties and Attractions," *Syracuse Journal* 4 April 1872.
2. Advertisement by Captain W. Swan, *Syracuse Journal* 20 July 1872.
3. "Picnic of the Onondaga Lake Club," *Syracuse Journal* 23 August 1873.
4. "The Sunday Exodus, *Syracuse Courier* 23 June 1879.
5. "How Many Syracusans Enjoy Themselves Across Onondaga Lake," *Syracuse Herald* 20 August 1899.
6. Sunday on the Lake," *Syracuse Courier* 27 June 1881.
7. "Along the Lake Shore," *Syracuse Standard* 16 June 1884.
8. "Along the Lake Shore."
9. "Sunday at the Lake." *Syracuse Courier* 13 June 1881.
10. "Outrage at Lake View," *Syracuse Courier* 12 August 1879.
11. "Outrage at Lake View."
12. A. J. Christopher, "Sketches of Yesterday, Lake View Point," *Baldwinsville News* 23 November 1961.
13. "Seek to Save Point on West Shore of Lake," *Syracuse Post Standard* 29 September 1929.
14. "Woman Awakened by Waste Lime Oozing Through Heating Register," *Syracuse Post Standard* 26 November 1943.
15. "Woman Awakened by Waste Lime Oozing Through Heating Register."
16. "While the Politicians Talked the Lake Began to Die," Robert W. Andrews, 3rd in a 5 part series, *Syracuse Post Standard* 16 October 1985.
17. "Solvay Process Gives State 400 Acres for Parking Lot, Scenic Area," *Syracuse Post Standard.* 29 December, 1953

6.1 Outing at Pleasant Beach pavillion, c. 1895, Onondaga Historical Association collection.

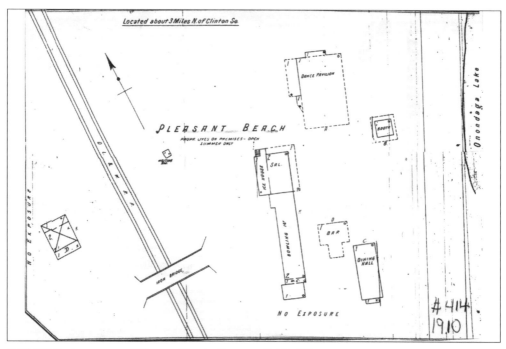

6.2 1910 Sanborn map of Pleasant Beach, Syracuse Public Library.

Many of the Onondaga Lake resorts would include a bowling alley, dance pavilion and a dining hall, often found inside of a hotel.

CHAPTER 6
COWAN'S GROVE,
LATER PLEASANT BEACH RESORT,
1874-1954

Cowan's Grove, later known as Pleasant Beach, boasted the reputation of having the best swimming beach on Onondaga Lake. It was located just north of Lake View Point, nestled in a small bay which provided the beach. This Onondaga Lake resort began in 1874, just two years after its neighbor Lake View Point. During the first two decades, Cowan's Grove did not seem to attract as thriving a business as Lake View. Newspaper articles mention crowds departing the lake steamer at Lake View, with only a few continuing on to Cowan's Grove for their picnic. In order to attract larger crowds, special events such as the Grand Military and Marine Engagement were held in 1877 to commemorate Commander Oliver Perry's 1813 victory over the British at the Battle of Lake Erie.

Cowan's Grove Becomes Pleasant Beach

When Willis S. Barnum and Alfred E. Aldridge took possession of Cowan's Grove in 1885, "it was a great mass of overgrown trees and brush, and there was about as much fun in going there as there would be in jumping off a house. They spent thousands of dollars in clearing out the grove, leveling off the beach, building restaurants, a bowling alley, dancing pavilion, bathing houses, etc. There's as much attraction at Pleasant Beach as there is at Sylvan Beach [Oneida Lake], and you can get there for just one-quarter the expenses."[1]

The two new owners complemented each other, as Mr. Aldridge had experience in the wholesale clam and oyster business supplying area hotels, and Willis Barnum had served as a first lieutenant in the Civil War and later had several business experiences. After two years of hard work remodeling Pleasant Beach, the grand opening was held in July 1887. The name of the resort was changed to make it more appealing to people seeking recreation.

In 1887, Syracusans could take a horse drawn car at the Empire House on Clinton Square, and go to the Salina Pier for passage on a steamer across Onondaga Lake for only twenty-five cents. The new owners built a great stone pier for the steamboats, with gates made of large timbers for safety, to hold back the crowds. If one wanted to get there in ten minutes, you could go to the DL&W depot to take a train going to Oswego, and get off at Pleasant Beach. The train ride also cost just twenty-five cents for the five-mile ride. For a while there was a fare war between the DL&W and the newly built Syracuse, Lakeside and Baldwinsville trolley line that made it cheaper to go to the lake than to stay home.

What did the new owners have available that would draw large crowds? On opening day one could watch yacht races from under a large shade tree, play baseball, try one's skill at pigeon shooting, rent a rowboat to catch whitefish, or just enjoy bathing at the best beach on Onondaga Lake. For decades, well into the 1940s, Pleasant Beach had coon and fox chases on the resort grounds where interested participants brought their own dogs for the hunt. The new owners built a double bowling alley with a grand promenade on top to enjoy the lake view. Clambakes were held with clams, "as only 'Al' Aldridge can furnish in Syracuse, and baked as only the people at Pleasant Beach can bake them."[2] A 'monstrous' dancing pavilion with a seven-piece orchestra led by Otto Drescher was ready for dancing during the day or evening throughout the summer. The new owners had a roller coaster built extending out over the shoreline to provide an added thrill.

Other attractions included a midway with games of chance, swings, and the Holmes tent, which was a photo studio where visitors could take home a souvenir of their day of fun. The resort provided thousands of rustic chairs and picnic tables for picnics, perhaps even more popular than now. At a children's zoo, "fox, deer, bear, and other harmless animals, perfectly tame, are added to make the children happy. Accommodations can be had for 500 horses in the newly erected open sheds. Uniform police maintain perfect order."[3] With this wide variety of attractions, soon Pleasant Beach was doubling the number of picnics booked compared to other Onondaga Lake resorts.

Pleasant Beach Has a Few Less Pleasant Moments

In order to attract even larger crowds to Pleasant Beach, daredevils performed parachute jumps from a hot air balloon over Onondaga Lake in clear view of thousands of spectators. On August 8, 1891, aeronaut De Ive was drowned after his parachute jump. Mr. Van Alstine of Liverpool, who was watching Mr. De Ive's descent that Sunday afternoon. . ."believes that the performer struck the water with such force that it knocked his breath out. . . . [The] Captain of the *Hiawatha*, the boat quickest to get to the parachute, says that De Ive motioned to the boats to come to him while he was 100 feet in the air."[4] Mr. Van Alstine and others worked well into Sunday night without recovering the body from the lake. It was not until Monday afternoon that Mr. Van Alstine was able to recover the body of Mr. De Ive, as crowds watched anxiously from the shore of Pleasant Beach. "Nothing was attached to the body and no scars were visible except those made by the grappling hooks. . . ."[5] It was theorized that the cause of drowning was the force with which he struck the surface of Onondaga Lake.

Professor De Ive was a thirty-five-year-old English stuntman, whose real name was James Buckingham. That August day he descended in front of 7,000 spectators at Pleasant Beach at about 6:00 PM. "He rose over Onondaga under a balloon, grasping a trapeze swing. He was supposed to perform by dropping into the water from a parachute mounted on the device. Instead, lines apparently tangled as he descended under the chute, crashing his body against the surface and burying him under the folds."[6]

Buckingham's family in England apparently never knew what had become of his body, until his great-granddaughter made inquiries in 1974. Onondaga County's Bureau of Vital Statistics determined that Mr. Buckingham was buried in the potter's field at Woodlawn Cemetery, either because his family in Lancashire, England, had been too poor to have his body returned home, or he had no known relatives. Thanks to reporter Dick Case, Mr. Buckingham's descendants now know where their ancestor is buried, after eighty-three years of thinking his body was never recovered from Onondaga Lake.

In July 1899, a sixteen-year-old youth, "was sitting with his sister and several other companions on a bench north of the rifle range. There was more or less firing at the range, but all at once the boy cried, 'I'm shot!' and placed his hand on the side of his neck."[7] At first his sister thought he was kidding until she saw blood trickling down her brother's neck, and then he fainted away. Initially it was thought the young man was killed, but he regained consciousness. The bullet had passed through the back of the neck, missing the spinal column and arteries by inches.

In the midst of the commotion at Pleasant Beach, the young man was placed on a Lakeside trolley to be brought to Syracuse. "The jar of the car and the severe pain made it necessary to remove him and he was taken home in a carriage."[8] The family hired a lawyer who argued that the shooting range was not properly constructed and that the proprietor, Mr. Aldridge, was liable for the accident. Mr. Aldridge refused to take responsibility for the shooting, arguing that there was nothing to show who fired the shot and that there were no serious results to the young man from the bullet wound.

Another uproar occurred on July 4, 1899, when one of the stars of the World's Columbian Exposition in Chicago, belly dancer Little Egypt, was scheduled to

6.3 Sketch of aeronaut De Ive's parachute jump in August 1891. By Andrew Thompson, 2000.

appear at Pleasant Beach. The clergy of Syracuse, already opposed to large crowds gathering on Sunday mornings at Onondaga Lake resorts, were shocked to learn that the star was scheduled to perform at Pleasant Beach. Fortunately for the resort, Little Egypt never appeared at Pleasant Beach, thus avoiding another standoff with area churches.

Little Egypt first shocked Victorian audiences at the 1893 Chicago World's Fair. Her belly dancing had previously been nearly unknown in the United States. Fairgoers did not mind that she was neither little nor Egyptian; her real name was Fahreda Mahzar, and she was Syrian. In a souvenir booklet of the World's Fair, it notes that Little Egypt and her friends were an instant success but that the Board of Lady Managers soon restricted her appearances at the fair. In spite of this restraint, belly dancers like Fahreda Mahzar and Catherine Devine, who claimed to be the original Little Egypt, continued to ride a crest of popularity on stages across the country.

Little Egypt

6.4 *(Left)* **Little Egypt, star from the Chicago Columbian Exposition. Picture from p. 14,** *The Serena Technique of Belly Dancing* **by Serena and Alan Wilson, Drake Publishers Inc., 1972, New York, N.Y.**

> ## PLEASANT BEACH.
> ### GEO. F. KNOWLES
> **WORLD'S FAIR MIDWAY PLAISANCE**
> **AND CONGRESS OF NATIONS.**
>
> Egyptians, Turks, Chinese, Japanese, Syrians, Bashi Bazooks, etc., etc.
> Also **"LITTLE EGYPT"** under her original manager, Geo. F. Knowles. This is the ORIGINAL AND ONLY Little Egypt.
> Herrmann, Champion Trick Bicyclist of the World.
> Special attractions for July 4th-Carlisle's Wild West and Knowles' Streets of Cairo.
> Admission to all, 10c.

6.5 *(Above)* **Pleasant Beach advertisement for World's Fair midway plaisance, p. 4,** *Syracuse Post Standard,* **July 1, 1899, Syracuse Public Library microfilm collection.**

Three Hotels Existed at Pleasant Beach

Why did Pleasant Beach Resort have so many hotels during its existence? The first hotel, the Lackawanna Hotel, shown below, burned to the ground. This picture, taken during 1890, shows a large three-story hotel with ornate balconies around it at every level. New trees have been planted in front of this portion of the hotel, evidence of the extensive upgrading done by the new owners of Pleasant Beach in 1885.

6.6 The first Pleasant Beach Hotel, the Lackawanna Hotel, c. 1890, Onondaga Co. Parks, Office of Museums

6.7 The Bob Johnson's Pleasant Beach Hotel, third Pleasant Beach Hotel, c. 1954, collection of Boberetta Johnson Albrigo.

The second hotel known as Reichert's Hotel, was demolished in 1915, when the lake level was raised by the construction of the New York State Barge Canal's new dam at Phoenix, only a few miles up the Oswego River. Reichert's catered to many annual outings and picnics, such as the Owls Social Club whose members relaxed on the hotel porch by indulging in Syracuse's famous Heberle's Congress Beer. The hotel, like most others on the lake, was noted for its fine food, especially the then most popular, "fish, frog and chicken dinners."[9]

When the latest hotel was built as a replacement for the second hotel, it was built into the side of a hill on land 100 yards further back from Onondaga Lake to avoid the likelihood of spring flooding caused by the lake's new dam at Phoenix. The third hotel was built in 1912 and was in continuous operation until

6.8 Camp Syracuse tents in back of chicken coops, postcard, author's collection.

1954, when it was torn down to make way for the new highway 690 that was built to connect the Thruway to the city of Syracuse. In later years, it was known as Bob Johnson's Pleasant Beach Hotel, and before a wrecking crew arrived to demolish the forty-two-year-old structure, Mr. Johnson invited 400 friends to a farewell party on July 27, 1954. "The friends started coming at 8. They came by automobile, on foot and by boat. Trolleys haven't run to Pleasant Beach in years. In addition to serving his last stock of liquors, Johnson brought in extra beer for the occasion . . . . In between a juke box blared out jive, jazz, Virginia reels and such songs as 'The Saga of Onondaga', especially recorded for the night."[10]

In an interview with Boberetta Johnson Albrigo during the summer of 2000, she told how her grandfather, Supply Sergeant Robert Alexander Johnson, was sent from the hills of West Virginia to the shores on Onondaga Lake in 1917 as a soldier stationed at Camp Syracuse. One Sunday morning the troops arrived and set up tents in the vegetable garden of the Nielezski family. The picture that follows shows the family's chicken coop with the soldiers' tents in the background. During Sergeant Johnson's stay at the camp prior to active duty during World War I, he met Mrs. Albrigo's grandmother, Lottie Nielezski, when he came up the hill to fetch water from the family's well. Mrs. Albrigo recalls her grandfather saying he had asked permission to take Lottie to Longbranch Park on at least one occasion. Before Sergeant Johnson went to Europe, the young couple eloped to New York City. Upon Johnson's return from war, the young couple left the region to find work. They later returned to buy the Pleasant Beach Resort during the early 1930s, where Johnson put his experience as a supply sergeant to work in catering to summer crowds.

During the summer of 2000, Mrs. Albrigo's neighbor, Anne Grovine, was also interviewed. She moved out to Lakeland with her parents in 1909. In the interview, she remembered that when she was about ten years old, she set up a roadside stand to sell apples for five cents apiece to the soldiers. Her two brothers wanted nothing to do with this adventure. The apples went into the soldiers' packs as they

6.9 Inspection at Camp Syracuse, Rudolph Bros., Art Publishers, Syracuse, N.Y., postmarked Aug. 12, 1918, author's collection.

prepared to go to the front in France. She also recalled her father taking her by the hand to watch free movies shown to both the soldiers and area residents. A large screen was set up on the hill coming up from Pleasant Beach and everyone would sit on the grass farther up the hill in the direction of State Fair Boulevard. Mrs. Grovine mentioned that a side benefit of Camp Syracuse to the Lakeland residents was that water pipes and electric service were brought to the area for the camp and eventually extended to the civilian residents.

The Pleasant Beach Resort site soon became famous and popular for its five dollar clambakes on weekends. When Mrs. Albrigo was fifteen, her grandfather allowed her to help out at the clambakes, but only at those for men and mixed groups; he considered the all-women's groups too rowdy and badly behaved for an impressionable young girl. Evidently the women used foul language and occasionally fights would occur. The clambakes began at noon, with Mrs. Johnson's homemade clam chowder, raw clams, salt potatoes, grilled hamburgers, and all the beverages, such as beer or soft drinks, that one could drink. At 2:30, liver and bacon were served, a dish popular then, but not common at today's clambakes and barbecues. Then at 5:00 PM dinner was served in the dance hall. This consisted of half a broiler chicken, steamed clams, red and white potatoes, and a dessert of homemade coffee cake. The clam broth was saved for the next bake, and Mrs. Albrigo remembers helping to cut up clams for the chowder. These very popular all-afternoon clambakes continued until fall, to be replaced by venison roasts when deer hunting season began.

The Prohibition Era, between 1920 and 1933, provided good times for Robert Johnson's Pleasant Beach Resort. The Eighteenth Amendment to the U.S. Constitution prohibited the manufacture, sale, and transportation of alcoholic beverages in the United States. Like many of his contemporaries, Johnson did not care for the prohibition laws, and he had the advantage of growing up in West

Virginia, where homemade whiskey, or moonshine, was commonly made. Robert produced homemade whiskey at his Baldwinsville farm, and through an understanding with the local authorities, avoided trouble. However, he was not quite so lucky with the federal prohibition agents, and narrowly escaped being caught on at least two occasions, according to family lore. One time, when he learned the federal authorities were coming, he dumped his batch of whiskey in nearby East Dead Creek, thus avoiding getting caught with it. However, had the feds stayed around until the next day, they would have noticed a number of very drunk chickens and cows staggering about after drinking from the creek! On another occasion, he actually was being pursued by the federal agents while driving his truck loaded to the hilt with illicit whiskey. He quickly drove into an old barn, but the rickety floor gave way under the weight of his load, and Robert, truck, whiskey and all, fell right through into the barn's basement! Evidently the agents couldn't find him, and he eluded capture once more.

The picture that follows shows the first clambake at Robert Johnson's Pleasant Beach Resort after World War II. The patrons were members of the Tyrol Club in 1945. During the 1940s, Pleasant Beach became known for its "chicken in the rough" suppers. This dish was popular well into the late 1960s in other area restaurants, and consisted of a bed of homemade French fries in a small basket, topped with half a chicken.

Inside Robert Johnson's Pleasant Beach Resort was the original mahogany bar from the earlier Lackawanna Hotel, and behind the bar a Syracuse University oar, signed by all the rowing team members, graced the wall. On April 6, 1950, the rowing shell capsized in a spring storm off Pleasant Beach, and Mr. Johnson brought the wet and chilled crew into the hotel where Lottie Johnson warmed them up

6.10 The Tyrol Club in front of Robert Johnson's Pleasant Beach Hotel, collection of Boberetta Johnson Albrigo.

with blankets, soup, and coffee royale. In appreciation, the team presented to the Johnsons the autographed oar with the following slogan, "Our Port in a Storm!"

For many years Onondaga Lake was famous for its catch of whitefish, a delicacy that was served at the Pleasant Beach Resorts as well as at the best hotels in New York City and throughout much of the United States around the turn of the twentieth century. At the farewell party for the resort's closing, Mr. Johnson shared the story of how during the previous summer, in 1953, a couple from New York City drove up to Onondaga Lake to catch the famous whitefish that they remembered savoring many years earlier. By 1953, the pollution had done its deadly work; there were no whitefish left, and all they caught were a few hardy carp.

In the end, the New York State Court of Claims paid Robert and Lottie Johnson $75,000 for four and a half acres of land needed to build Route 690. The land taken by the state included, "a main house and tavern, rest rooms, garage, and open bar building, [and] tap building to store beer."[11]

This was small compensation for a successful Onondaga Lake resort that had lasted about eighty years, from the golden age of Onondaga Lake resorts until modern progress in the form of highway construction that brought its demise. In its first decades, Pleasant Beach did not attract large numbers until its new owners regenerated the resort into one of the leading crowd pleasers on the lake. This was done by developing a wide range of attractions that would draw large crowds. Pleasant Beach was one of the first to take the Onondaga Lake resort industry to the next stage of development, later copied by the Maple Bay Resort in the early 1890s.

Notes

1. "Out at Pleasant Beach, There Was a Grand Time Monday at the Formal Opening," *Syracuse Times* 9 July 1887.

2. "Out at Pleasant Beach, There Was a Grand Time Monday at the Formal Opening."

3. "Pleasant Beach," *Baldwinsville Era* 1 June 1889.

4. "The Body Dragged Up," *Syracuse Courier*, 18 August 1891.

5. "The Body Dragged Up."

6. Richard G. Case, "Aeronaut Buried in City's Potter's Field," *Syracuse Herald American*, 10 Nov. 1974.

7. "Shot at Pleasant Beach, Harry Tischler Asks One Thousand Dollars, "*Syracuse Post Standard*, 23 July 1899.

8. "Shot at Pleasant Beach, Harry Tischler Asks One Thousand Dollars. "

9. Joseph Wentworth, "As it Was–Onondaga Lake," *North Syracuse Star News*, 6 May 1981.

10. "Last Pleasant Beach Hotel Closes Doors," *Syracuse Herald Journal*, 28 July 1954.

11. "Extra Paid for Land on Lake Shore," *Syracuse Herald Journal*, 5 April 1957.

7.1 The Rockaway complex of bowling alleys, hotel, and Zetts Bar, 1899. Syracuse Souvenir booklet published by Chamber of Commerce, author's collection.

This is the view one would get of the Rockaway Resort as you arrived for the day by steamer and would dock at the end of the long pier. This one-of-a-kind picture was part of the 1899 Syracuse Souvenir booklet that was published by the Chamber of Commerce. The Rockaway was open for business year around, as it was the meeting place for the Onondaga Ice Yacht Club that raced their iceboats in front of the resort.

7.2 Advertisement for Onondaga Lake resorts including the Maine, *Syracuse Courier*, July 1, 1904, from Syracuse Public Library microfilm collection.

CHAPTER 7
ROCKAWAY BEACH AND SOME SMALLER RESORTS

The Smaller Resorts of Onondaga Lake

Traveling north along the west shore from Pleasant Beach, the next two resorts were Manhattan Beach and Rockaway Beach. Manhattan Beach was one of several minor establishments around Onondaga Lake that did not offer large-scale amusements and recreation. "Consisting of a hotel and wading beach, it intended to compete with the larger complexes on the lake. Unfortunately, this was not the case. Manhattan Beach was one of the first to disappear." [1]

Near the close of the 1890s, Rosey (John) Miller opened a resort known as "the Maine," just east of Long Branch where the Seneca River outlet meets Onondaga Lake. The Maine was a catchy name for a resort, so soon after the Spanish American War in which the American ship the *USS Maine* was destroyed in Havana harbor, Cuba. This modest resort consisted of a small hotel and a boat livery that catered to fishermen. Later the Maine was operated by Judd (William) Mason. This July 1, 1904, advertisement by Mike Gaffney announces that a fish fry accompanied by cold lager beer will be served at all hours at the resort.

Stuhler's Tavern and Zea Breeze Tavern were located in the same vicinity as the Maine, and were places that catered to men. In these taverns, "a man could get away from it all and enjoy a free lunch with his nickel beer." [2] Rarely did women frequent these establishments and, "those who ventured in with their male escort were not looked upon too kindly." [3]

What Made the Rockaway Unique?

In 1892, Captain John J. Hecker, a Civil War veteran, purchased the hotel at Rockaway from the Cowans. The Cowan deed to the place dated back to 1855, and as early as 1885, public bathing facilities were available. In the *Syracuse Journal* of July 23, 1885, a short advertisement for Rockaway Beach stated, "Good wide beach, very sloping, no danger. New dressing rooms and suits for Ladies and Gents. Price 25 cents." [4]

In many ways, Rockaway Beach was much like the other Onondaga Lake resorts of the 1890s, offering a shady picnic grove, clambakes, a dancing pavilion, bowling alleys, a baseball diamond, and the best fishing to be had on the lake. It was only five and a half miles from Syracuse, stop number nine on the trolley line to Oswego. It did have a large playground for children with swings and other games, but it had little in the way of amusement rides like Pleasant Beach, Maple Bay, and Long Branch Park. In general, Rockaway never intended to compete with the other larger summer resorts on the west shore of Onondaga Lake. Mr. Hecker sought to attract adult customers, particularly sportsmen, by offering unique meals and by being open the entire year.

This 1910 Sanborn map illustrates the simple layout of Rockaway Beach, which included the bowling alleys, the hotel and saloon, the dance pavilion, and several outbuildings. The adjacent 1890s photo of the Rockaway shows the Zetts Brewery Saloon next to the hotel. Smoke can be seen coming from the booth on the far right of the picture. Note the women wearing their Gibson Girl style hats, and typical turn-of-the-century dresses in front of the hotel. The Rockaway was renowned for its clambakes, and that may be what is producing the steam on the right of the picture. These clambakes were not the run-of-the-mill 'steamer' variety, but real bakes, "with a hot stone pad heaped with stuffed chicken, corn and clams. The entire lot was covered with canvas, topped with sand and left to bake using the heat from the stone."[5]

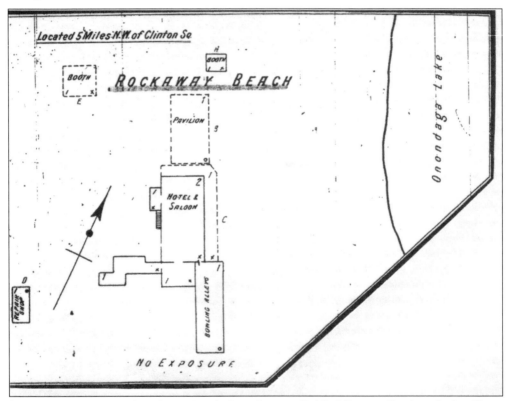

7.3 1910 Sanborn map of Rockaway Beach, from Syracuse Public Library collection of microfilm.

The Rockaway catered to church picnics, sportsmen's banquets, and other private parties. At the hotel restaurant guests enjoyed their Sunday dinner including chicken, frog's legs, Onondaga Lake whitefish, and samphire. Samphire is a native salt marsh plant similar to asparagus that was picked and served as a local delicacy at area restaurants. The Onondaga whitefish was another delicacy popular around the lake and also was served at Delmonico's Restaurant in New York City (by name). During the first decade of the twentieth century, the Rockaway served a wild duck dinner for only twenty-five cents, which included consommé, potato, and vegetable. The ducks were sure to be fresh, as they had been shot the same

7.4 Photograph of Rockaway Beach with adjoining Zetts Lager Saloon, 1890s, Onondaga County Parks Office of Museums.

day by Mr. Hecker or his son Joseph Jr. right on the hotel's property. When Dick Long interviewed the daughter of Joe Hecker Jr., Mrs. William Roberts, she remembered, "Father and my uncles would go hunting around the shore and would come back with enough mallard ducks to feed nearly two hundred people. People said it was the marl [clay silt from the lake bed] on the shore that attracted the ducks."[6] In this picture, taken in 1910, Joseph Hecker Jr. proudly displays the results of the morning's hunt, which was to be served to hotel guests for dinner later that day.

7.5 Photograph of Joseph Hecker Jr. standing in front of ducks, Rockaway Beach Hotel, 1910, Onondaga County Parks, Office of Museums.

During the late nineteenth century, many of the local Syracuse breweries, such as Heberle, Greenway, and Zetts had special arrangements to sell beer at the west shore resorts on Onondaga Lake. According to June Hecker, the widow of Jacob Hecker's son, George, Zetts Lager was the brand sold at Rockaway Beach, because Xavier Zetts' granddaughter, Louise, was married to Jacob Hecker, one of the five Hecker brothers. The Zetts Brewery Building is one of the few local nineteenth century breweries still standing on the north side of Syracuse. This 1890s close-up picture shows the 'typical' crowd in front of the George Zetts Lager Beer Saloon, which was attached to the Rockaway Hotel. It is a mixed crowd, including someone's dog.

7.6 Photograph of close-up of Zetts Saloon at Rockaway Beach, 1890s, Onondaga County Parks, Office of Museums.

The Hecker family consisted of five brothers: Joseph, Jacob, John, Valentine, and Anthony, as well as a sister, Mame. The picture that follows show three of the brothers who worked at Rockaway Beach. Anthony, or Sully, is on the far left, Val is on the far right, and the owner of the resort, Joseph, is pictured in the center wearing a black waistcoat.

Rockaway, Home of the Ice Yachtsmen and Fox Chases

During the cold winter months, the activity at the Rockaway did not cease. Iceboating and fox and rabbit chases were two principle outdoor activities headquartered at the Rockaway Hotel. During the morning of the fox hunt, a man on horseback would drag a piece of fresh meat over the nearby swamps and ice to the northern end of the lake. When all was ready, the dogs were let loose, stampeding and yelping as they ran with their noses to the frozen ground. The mostly male crowd would bet on which dog would reach the bait first.

7.7 **The Hecker brothers on steps of hotel, collection of June Hecker.**

On February 11, 1912, under the auspices of the Hunters' Club of Onondaga, as many as two thousand sportsmen braved the extreme cold to attend the sports carnival at Rockaway Beach. "In the first rabbit chase there were 17 [hound dog] entries, and first prize was taken by Bugle, owned by Thomas Hughes of this village [Skaneateles]."[7]

7.8 **The winter rabbit chase, hunters with their dogs in front of hotel, early-twentieth century, collection of Boberetta Johnson Albrigo.**

During the turn of the twentieth century, iceboating was one of Onondaga Lake's most distinctive winter sports, and the Rockaway was the headquarters for the Onondaga Ice Yacht Club. In those days, when cars averaged a top speed of twenty to forty miles per hour, ice yachting was particularly thrilling, as a well-designed iceboat could exceed sixty miles per hour. This 1905 picture is one the Onondaga Lake's well-known iceboats, the *Rockaway*.

7.9 The Rockaway **iceboat, early twentieth century, Onondaga Co. Parks Office of Museums.**

Iceboating on Onondaga Lake goes back to 1888 when Reuben Thurwachter built his first ice yacht called the *Scud*. Soon after, the people of Liverpool took up this exciting sport. Thurwachter first had experience sailing an iceboat on the Hudson River near Poughkeepsie. The boats were very streamlined with slim runners that could travel at lightning speeds when the ice was smooth and free from snow. When there was a strong wind, Thurwachter sailed his trim craft *Best Girl* from the outlet on Onondaga Lake to the Iron Pier. He sailed the entire length of the lake in five minutes flat. By the end of the nineteenth century there were twelve or thirteen ice crafts on the lake every winter afternoon, and by 1901, that number had increased to about twenty-five. Each craft was built differently. The size of the canvas sail would vary from 200 to well over 300 feet. The length of the craft ranged from 16 to over 35 feet, and various types of wood were used, such as redwood, ash, and walnut.

Captain Hecker and his sons grew interested in the sport through Mr. Thurwachter in the winter of 1899-1900. On February 5, 1899, in the *Syracuse Journal* article, J. Dan Ackerman wrote, "It is easily seen that the sport is gaining in interest and will soon be the most popular winter recreation. Most of the ice yachts on the lake have their anchorage at Rockaway Beach and every afternoon the resort is the scene of a merry gathering of ice yacht enthusiasts. The Baldwinsville and Lakeside

Railway Company is also becoming interested in the promotion of the sport, and manager Newton has announced his intention of putting up a trophy in the shape of a silver cup to be contested for by the different yachts on the lake."[8]

By the winter of 1901, the Onondaga Lake Ice Yacht Club, only one year old, had 100 members. Reuben C. Thurwachter was the commodore of the fleet. During the winter of 1899-1900, Thurwachter's *Best Girl* won the championship cup and pennant. For the 1900-1901 season, more races were planned, and several cups and silk pennants would be awarded to race winners. For the new ice yacht season, John Hecker had his boat *Rockaway* re-rigged to better compete with the other boats. "She has been lengthened to 29 feet overall, with 287 square feet of sail. A new runner plank and new set of sails are the other additions to the *Rockaway*, conceded to be second in speed to but one boat on the lake."[9]

Many of the iceboats had colorful local names such as *Blizzard, Sodyash, Little Devil, Dutch, Exciter,* and *Alternator,* the largest craft on the lake in 1899. The owners raced every Sunday during the winter in front of the Rockaway. Ice yachting parties became the fad in social circles, and at times special cars were put into service on the Lakeside trolley line to transport people to the Rockaway. The top floor of the hotel was the Onondaga Ice Yacht Club's meeting place, and here the trophies were displayed in glass cases along the wall. Captain Hecker Sr. often served a turkey dinner to club members following the meeting.

In the same 1901 article previously quoted, it was noted that no serious accidents had occurred on Onondaga Lake up to that point. One of the worst dangers to befall an iceboater would be stretches of open water caused by thaws, ice harvesting, or by running water from small creeks emptying into the lake. This old photo illustrates how ice was harvested from Onondaga Lake until 1901. Ice harvesting was discontinued as early as 1901 due to health concerns over the increasing pollution of the lake. The men used saws to cut through the ice, and the ice chunks were floated to nearby sleds to be removed to icehouses, where the ice was packed in sawdust for summer use by the lake resorts. After harvesting, the large areas of open water

7.10 Ice harvesting on Onondaga Lake, circa 1900, Onondaga Co. Parks Office of Museums.

left became extremely dangerous for the iceboats. Because of the lightning speed of the crafts, it was often too late to avoid the open water that could cause death within minutes. Other times, sudden squalls would lift one runner clear off the ice, dumping the driver, and then the craft would continue on as a runaway until it overturned or crashed along the shoreline.

Finally in 1904 the worst happened. Three people were killed in an iceboat collision on Onondaga Lake. The victims were Charles Markham, James Jackson, and George Todd, all associated with the Ice Yacht Club at the Rockaway. After this Sunday tragedy, club members just sat around in gloom and shock in the upstairs meeting room of the hotel, with no desire to go out again onto the ice for another spin.

This is a later version of *Best Girl* owned by Jacob Hecker, the brother of Joseph. In spite of accidents, iceboat racing remained popular through the 1920s, providing a thrilling high-speed ride, and socializing after the races at the Rockaway.

7.11 *The Best Girl* iceboat, circa 1927, collection of June Hecker.

Diary Helps to Record Daily Occurrences

From 1907 to 1912 Joseph Hecker Sr. kept a diary, particularly during the winter months, and today it provides glimpses of the life at the Rockaway. In a 1954 *Syracuse Herald American* article, Dick Long recounts some of Hecker's diary entries describing ducks returning in March and the cat having kittens in April. During April, the spring-summer season party bookings at the Rockaway seemed to pick up. On Sunday, May 3, 1908, Mr. Hecker wrote, "a clambake–39 people–a jolly crowd."[10] During the days before the Intercollegiate Regatta races on Saturday, May 23, 1908, he mentioned, "university crew won from Middies, U.S.N., by length and a half."[11] The next day he recorded, "A fine crowd–run out of fish–baseball game, temperature was 75 degrees."[12]

As with the Pleasant Beach Hotel, in 1915, the Rockaway Hotel had to be moved back 400 yards from the lake because the new dam at Phoenix raised the lake level for the new large canal. The north side of the hotel had to be removed before the rest of the hotel could be moved to the hill farther from the lake.

During the 1920s and 1930s, the Rockaway Beach Hotel was the object of raids by the police for gambling activities and for serving alcohol during the Prohibition Era. In early June 1924, on a tip from some women who complained to New York State troopers that their husbands had lost money in games of chance, the police raided Joseph Hecker Jr's Rockaway Hotel at 2:00 AM. They were unable to find evidence of high-stakes gambling and ended up seizing only a quarter slot machine. The money from the slot machine was later turned over to the poor fund of the Town of Geddes. The newspaper reported that, "Men and women rushed helter-skelter into the darkness at 2 o'clock yesterday morning. . . . Several women, who were seated at tables with a number of men, jumped up, grabbed their wraps and disappeared, fearing the troopers intended to jot down their names."[13]

On May 13, 1931, the Rockaway Hotel was again raided, this time by a squad of Syracuse federal prohibition agents. They found a barrel and a half of beer and arrested Joseph Hecker Jr., who was summoned before a United States commission.

By 1954, the Rockaway Beach Hotel was still standing after almost sixty years of use, but now the old top floor trophy room was an apartment for Mrs. Helen Colvin, the mother-in-law of Mrs. Ellis Hecker Roberts. The bottom floor had been subdivided into several small apartments, so no longer were guests from Syracuse welcomed to the sumptuous meals of the past in the hotel's dining room.

Late during the summer of 1954, the wrecker's bulldozer leveled the structure for the new Route 690 that connected motorists from the Thruway to downtown Syracuse. Today, Route 690 passes right over the rubble of the old hotel, and two toppled concrete columns lay near the shore of Onondaga Lake where the remains of Rockaway Beach's crumbled pier lie on the lake bottom. These two concrete columns are the only architectural evidence of what was one of the most unique resorts on Onondaga Lake.

Notes

1. Christine K. Shephard, "Where the Resorts Were," *Liverpool Courier* 31 August 1992.
2. Shephard, "Where the Resorts Were."
3. Shephard, "Where the Resorts Were."
4. "Summer Resorts Bathing at Rockaway Beach," *Syracuse Journal,* 23 July 1885.
5. Shephard, "Where the Resorts Were."
6. Dick Long, "Lakeshore Survivors Tell of Onondaga's Gay Old Days," *Syracuse Herald American,* 4 April 1954.
7. "Skaneateles Dogs Win Prizes," *Marcellus Observer* 16 February 1912.
8. J. Dan Ackerman, "Ice Yachting is Exciting Sport," *Syracuse Journal,* 5 February 1899.
9. "Ice Yachts Ready to Go," *Syracuse Post Standard,* 23 September 1901.
10. Long, "Lakeshore Survivors Tell of Onondaga's Gay Old Days."
11. Long, "Lakeshore Survivors Tell of Onondaga's Gay Old Days."
12. Long, "Lakeshore Survivors Tell of Onondaga's Gay Old Days."
13. "Troopers Raid Hecker's Hotel," *Syracuse Post Standard,* 2 June 1924.

MAPLE BAY.
A Summer Resort on Onondaga Lake.—George D. Goddard, Syracuse, N. Y.
34

8.1 **Five-picture composite views of Maple Bay 1899, Syracuse Souvenir Booklet, published by Chamber of Commerce, p. 34, author's collection.**

The Maple Bay Resort on Onondaga Lake was known as "The King of All Summer Resorts." These five photos published in the 1899 Syracuse Souvenir Booklet by the Chamber of Commerce show the large hotel, dance pavilion, the wild animal cage and 300-foot-long pier with a steamer unloading passengers. In the lower right corner resorters are walking up from the trolley stop.

CHAPTER 8
MAPLE BAY,
LATER LAKESIDE PARK

The King of All Summer Resorts

Maple Bay is located on an alcove in Onondaga Lake's northern shore, just west of the lake outlet. The Maple Bay Resort was established in 1889 at the point where the curve straightens out and the actual west shore begins. The shore around the alcove was covered with dense maple woods, thus giving this resort its first name. Mr. Willis S. Barnum, one of the former proprietors of Pleasant Beach, bought this shore property in 1889 from Mr. Winchell and Mr. Brand. He employed a team of carpenters to construct a 100 by 32 foot pavilion and another building, 98 by 45 feet. According to a brief article in the March 21, 1889, *Baldwinsville Gazette*, the buildings were scheduled for completion by June 1, 1889. Proprietor Willis S. Barnum had a major hotel built on the site in 1890, and by the following year Maple Bay boasted in the local newspapers that it was, "The King of All Summer Resorts." This circa 1890 picture shows the hotel and bathhouse, that were the start of the Maple Bay Resort.

8.2 **Maple Bay Hotel and adjacent buildings, 1894, Onondaga Historical Association Collection.**

The 1891 advertisement went on to say, "Easily reached by DL&W Railroad or by steamers from Geddes Pier or Iron Pier. The largest grove on the lake, cool and shady, and watered with cold spring water. . . . Fine hotel where the finest dinners in Central New York can be procured. . . . The museum is an object of interest to all . . . . The pier is the largest on the lake. Uniformed police on the grounds at all times."[1]

During the 1890s Maple Bay became known for its superb dinners served at the hotel. As with the other Onondaga resorts, they catered to excursions by various social organizations. On August 28, 1890, the Knights of Pythias held their annual field day at Maple Bay, traveling from Syracuse on the Oswego division of the DL&W Railroad. The illustrations that follow include the menu that was prepared for the Knights of Pythias in 1890, and another menu which was published in the August 16, 1891, *Syracuse Times.* The 1890 menu does not include anything unfamiliar to us today, but the later menu of 1891 had a French flair and includes some interesting items such as mock turtle soup, and Saratoga chips, potato chips first created in Saratoga Springs, New York. Also on this menu were calf's bowl and French kisses for dessert, most likely a meringue or confection.

At the end of the 1890 summer season, the Syracuse Merchant Tailors Exchange held their annual clambake at Maple Bay at a cost of two dollars per ticket. Maple Bay/Lakeside Park hired Colonel Ephraim Thurber from Providence, Rhode Island, to prepare the clambake in the traditional style of his father. He had barrels of seaweed shipped to Lakeside Park especially for this outing. A large bon-

---

Excursions of the Knights of Pythias To-day
August 28, 1890

The Syracuse Knights of Pythias hold their annual excursion and field day at Maple Bay to-day. Knights are expected from neighboring towns. The Oswego division run an excursion train to the lake at 7:45 this morning, and the uniformed rank of the Syracuse division leave at 2' o'clock this afternoon for the Bay.

Dinner will be taken at the Maple Bay Hotel, The following being the bill of fare:

Carte de Joure.

SOUP.
Consomme,   Dom Pedro,
Cream of Green Corn.
FISH.
Broiled Salmon Maitre Hotel.
ROASTS.
Beef,   Lamb,   Chicken.
VEGETABLES.
Boiled Potatoes,   Mashed Potatoes,
Green Corn, Green Peas, Beets.
PASTRY.
Apple Pie,   Blackberry Pie.
Assorted Cakes.
DESSERT.
Ice Cream,   Watermelon,
Tea,   Coffee.

At Maple Bay From 4 to 8 P.M. To-Day.
August 16, 1891

CARTE DU JOUR.
Little Neck Clams.
POTAGES
Mock Turtle,   Consomme Julienne.
POISSONS
Filet of Halibut, drawn butter sauce.
Broiled Blue.   Potato Croquettes.
Saratoga Chips.   Tomato.   Celery.
Cucumber.   Broiled Lobster, with lemon.
ENTREES.
Broiled Spring Chicken on Toast.
Calf's bowl, with Mushrooms.
Les Petites Pates aux Huitres.
Imperial Punch.
ROTIS
Prime Ribs of Chicago Beef. Brown Potatoes.
Leg of Mutton. Currant Jelly.
Saddle of Veal, with Carrots.
Sherry Wine, Russe Jelly.
LEGUMES.
Boiled Potatoes.   Sweet Potatoes.
Mashed Potatoes.
Asparagus.   Refugee String Beans.
Green Peas.
SUCRES.
Banana Shortcake.
Green Apple Pie.   Lady-Fingers.
Watermelon.   Strawberry Ice Cream.
French Kisses.
Demi-tasse.   Macaroons.

8.3 Menus from Maple Bay Hotel, 1890 and 1891, Syracuse Public Library microfilm collection of newspapers.

fire was lit and allowed to burn down to ashes, upon which the seaweed was placed. "On top of this sizzling bed of salty grass were dumped the clams, the lobsters, the corn, the potatoes, the fish and the chicken. Before the tarpaulin could be spread over the pile, the incense from it began to permeate the atmosphere [when everything was ready]. There was no speechmaking. Everybody was bent on filling the vacuum under his belt."[2]

By the fall of 1891, Willis S. Barnum was still busy organizing harvest moon excursions of people from Geddes Pier on the south shore to Maple Bay on the north shore of Onondaga Lake. The group of about sixty people left the pier at eight in the evening and for about two hours enjoyed the beautiful early autumn night on the lake, before the merry party went on to Maple Bay. The group, "spread the tables, filled with good things brought with them, host Barnum furnished the coffee, and after satisfying their hunger and thirst they sped away to the dancing platform. Astrello's orchestra furnished music, and until after midnight the party enjoyed themselves hugely dancing, rolling ten pins, etc. A delightful [trolley] ride around the lake, their special train landed them home again about 1:30 this morning."[3]

It was during the last decade of the nineteenth century that more and more pleasure seekers arrived at the three hundred-foot-long pier, the longest on the lake, to enjoy the growing number of attractions at the one hundred-acre resort. Livery rowboats could be rented for twenty-five cents for the first hour and fifteen cents for every hour thereafter. The picnic grounds could accommodate up to twenty thousand people, and there were activities and attractions to interest all ages. To keep children entertained, there was a small menagerie, including a bear, animal rides, a miniature train ride, a nickelodeon, a giant carousel, and a roller coaster that appealed to all ages. As time went on a roller-skating rink and a bicycle track were added, and plans were made for tennis courts.

As early as August 1890, W. S. Barnum was described as a hustler, as he promoted ambitious plans to increase the popularity of his resort. He campaigned to have Maple Bay become the permanent location of the New York State shooting competition and secured support from numerous Central New York gun clubs. He also wanted to build a clubhouse at Maple Bay for the Syracuse Amateur Athletic Club as soon as possible, "[It] will be built on the shore of the lake, and a half-mile track for racing of all kinds will be laid out. The new club house will be 60 x 24 feet and two stories high."[4]

In the mid-1890s, Mr. Adam Ecker leased the grounds and buildings at Maple Bay for several years, booking a long list of different attractions. He scheduled comedy sketches, balloon ascensions over the lake, and a high wire bicyclist. In one such exhibition, Professor Raut was scheduled to ascend to a height of over two thousand feet and then parachute to the lake's surface. The Syracuse newspapers reassured readers that the Volunteer Life Saving Corps. would be in readiness to pick him up when he came down. Balloon ascensions were very popular all during the 1890s as the American public became interested in flight. Fatal accidents sometimes occurred, however, such as the one near Pleasant Beach in 1891. In July 1899, Professor Phelps made a parachute jump from a balloon at 1,100 feet before a crowd of 1,500 people without mishap. The advertisement that follows appeared in the *Syracuse Post Standard* on July 15, 1899, making it known that this event was free of charge for the patrons of the Syracuse, Lakeside and Baldwinsville Railroad.

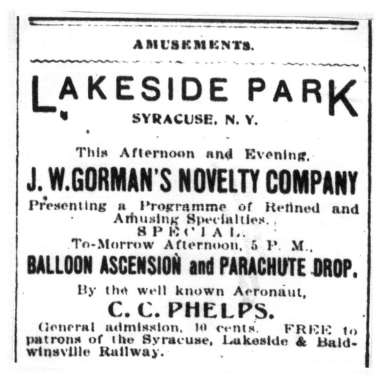

8.4 Advertisement for balloon ascension and parachute drop, *Syracuse Post Standard*, July 15, 1899, Syracuse Public Library microfilm collection.

The Open Air Rustic Theater

In the spring of 1899, Mr. J. W. Gorman, manager of the Gorman Amusement Company of Boston, was hired by the Syracuse, Lakeside and Baldwinsville Railroad Company to construct a rustic theater just south of Maple Bay or Lakeside Park, the new name for the resort. "The theater will be an open air affair and will be something of a novelty in this part of the state. It will have a seating capacity of 2,500 and admission will be free to patrons of the road. Vaudeville performances will be given daily." [5] The firm that Mr. Gorman managed had been involved in building and managing twenty-two different parks in 1898 from Bangor, Maine, to Pittsburgh.

The opening of the Rustic Theater coincided with the extension of the streetcar service to Maple Bay. The structure was nestled in the maple grove, a lovely rural setting, and was open on all sides except for the dressing rooms in the rear of the stage. Inside a railing were raised seats for about five hundred people and for which a small admission was charged. Outside the railing were additional seats that had a clear view of the stage. Only soft drinks were served inside the theater.

Mr. H. S. Newton, the general manager of the trolley line, planned to offer only high-class vaudeville entertainment to attract entire families. Opening was June 19, 1899, when J. H. Gorman's Olympia Company performed to a large audience. Vaudeville acts were popular in New England and Gorman actively promoted various companies and acts in Central New York, including the Cosmopolitans, Howards Comique Novelty Company, and the London Vaudeville Company. A typical repertoire included comic sketches, dancers, singers, acrobatic acts, and trained dogs, but the entertainment was described as clean as well as amusing.

Later during the summer of 1899, the thirty member Russian Imperial Court Band performed from 3:00 in the afternoon until 7:00 in the evening. A news article promoted the band as having, "an excellent reputation in all of the large European cities where it has appeared. . . . In connection with the band concert there will be the American cinematograph pictures which aroused so much favorable comment last week among those who patronized the Lakeside Theater."[6] A cinematograph was an early motion picture projector which showed silent movies often accompanied by music.

As newer forms of entertainment were developed—namely, silent movies and recordings—Lakeside Park offered its patrons the latest innovation, gram-o-phon-a-scope entertainment, described as "a modification of the gramophone that portrays scenes and living pictures."[7] For example, as pictures of the Old Grace Church in New York City were shown, the Grace Church choir would be heard singing, "Abide With Me."

8.5 Advertisement for "the gram-o-phon-o-scope," *Syracuse Post Standard*, August 19, 1899, Syracuse Public Library microfilm collection.

On a daily basis, the Syracuse, Lakeside and Baldwinsville Railroad took passengers to the open-air rustic theater every seven minutes during the summer months. On July 14, 1899, a special event at Lakeside Park included a famous vaudeville company at the theater and a grand fireworks display by "Pain, the Fireworks King." The advertisement that follows appeared in the *Syracuse Post Standard* the day of the event and ends with the statement, "without fail this time," suggesting they got rained out earlier in July.

8.6 Advertisement for "Pain, The Fireworks King," *Syracuse Post Standard,* **August 3, 1899, Syracuse Public Library microfilm collection.**

The next day, the papers estimated that twelve thousand people attended the fireworks display, the largest gathering of people at one resort on the west shore of Onondaga Lake. Most of the onlookers came from Syracuse via the streetcars or the steamboat, and the event was delayed so hundreds of people could complete their eight-mile journey to the bay. Before 6:00 PM, people were waiting in Clinton Square to board the trolleys, with many giving up on the trolley and deciding instead to go by carriages or bicycles down 'the Boulevard' to Maple Bay. Two strings of carriages and bikes extended as far back to Pleasant Beach, and the resort grounds soon became a mass of humanity waiting for the fireworks to start. The newspaper accounts reported that the crowds were good-natured: "the thrifty housewife is putting up jam. As the man in the vaudeville says those who had soft boiled eggs for supper had them scrambled by the time they reached Lakeside."[8]

To try to accommodate the large crowds, the Syracuse, Lakeside and Baldwinsville Railroad had twelve big cars, four double deckers and eight trailers ready, but this proved inadequate. The double deckers, like the one shown below, each carried about two hundred people, and each of the big motorcars and trailers could carry about half that number. The car shown was one of seven the SL&B Railroad Company owned in 1899. All were discontinued by 1907. They were too heavy for the bridges when fully loaded, and at major events it took too long for people to embark and disembark from double deckers.

The fireworks display was a huge success and a product of its time, coming only a year after the Spanish American War. The fireworks show started at 9:30 PM, with preliminary balloons and floats that lighted up the water, followed by bombs and rockets that greatly pleased the crowd but frightened horses, which unharnessed themselves from the carriages and proceeded back to Syracuse without

8.7 Photo of SL&B double-decker trolley, 1899. Syracuse souvenir booklet published by the Syracuse Chamber of Commerce, p. 15, author's collection.

their owners. The lakefront crowd gave resounding applause to the display, but "the chief event of the night was a representation of the Battle of Santiago, which was pictured on the water a couple of hundred feet from the pier. While the lake was illuminated for over a mile around the floating light, a representation of a Spanish boat emerging from the harbor was given. Almost simultaneously was shown an American boat approaching from the opposite side. Fire was opened by the latter and in an instant balls of fire were hurling back and forth and then followed the explosion. The Spanish floats were blown to atoms and then there was tumultuous applause. The applause was continued when a life size portrait of Admiral Dewey, 25 by 30 feet, was shown."[9]

8.8 Sketch of fireworks display while steamboats were arriving, by Andrew Thompson.

While Steamboats Were Still Arriving

The great event of July 14, 1899, ended without incident, with the majority of the crowd making it back to the city by midnight. Besides the complex fireworks display, up to four thousand people were able to enjoy the vaudeville acts held at the Rustic Theater, either seated inside or crowding around outside the theater. During the course of the fireworks display, Iron Pier steamboats were still arriving at the long pier in spite of being, "warned that they must land passengers only at their own risk,"[10] but there were no accidents. On the return trip to the city, some of the double decker trolleys carried up to 275 passengers, but there was little rowdiness, except for some minor incidents.

Because the fireworks display was so successful in July, Lakeside Park had Mr. Pain, the fireworks king, make return visit in early August. This time themes from the recently concluded Spanish American War were again greeted with the applause of about ten thousand people. One accident occurred when a young man was knocked down by a horse that had been frightened by the aerial displays. One interesting sidelight of the giant fireworks display was the presence of Game Protector William Everson at Maple Bay to see that, "no dynamite exploded in Onondaga Lake during the exhibition of Pain's fireworks."[11]

8.9 Sketch of wire-enclosed building containing wild animals, by Theresa Russo, art teacher at East Syracuse-Minoa school district.

As representative of the Anglers' Association of Onondaga Lake, Everson's concern was the possibility the fireworks might kill the fish, thus adversely affecting sport fishing in the lake. After he spoke with W. F. Terry, Mr. Pain's representative, Mr. Terry decided it was best to abandon the idea of a submarine display involving explosives. Mr. Terry commented however, "There is very little water at the point where we propose to have this exhibit and the talk about killing fish is amusing."[12] The concern at that time appears not to have been primarily environmental, but rather to ensure sport fishing was not spoiled.

Monkeyshines, Novelties, and Rough Riders

During the spring of 1896 a group of Philadelphia capitalists enlarged Maple Bay by building a gigantic carousel, lawn tennis courts, an immense Shoot-the-Chutes, a roller skating rink and a half-mile bicycle track with a three thousand-seat grandstand facing the Rustic Theater. The new management built a small zoo for the enjoyment of children, but young and old alike came to the wire-enclosed building to watch monkeys, peacocks, and other species, although, "ladies with feathers in their hats usually gave the zoo a wide berth, fearing a long monkey's arm might reach through the fence and damage their millinery."[13] The sketch on page 98 shows curious passers-by looking at the huge wild animal enclosure.

The Rustic Theater was an investment of the Syracuse, Lakeside and Baldwinsville Railroad and booked a great variety of entertainment. When people completed their trolley ride to Maple Bay, they had a coupon attached to their streetcar ticket, which entitled them to free admission to the hippodrome or silent movie theater. This coupon was called a novelty, and adults not interested in the picture shows or shows by the many vaudeville companies could easily find young people willing to use their novelty coupons.

In August 1899, Mr. Mason Mitchell presented an illustrated lecture about his experiences with Roosevelt's Rough Riders in the Spanish American War of 1898.

8.10 Advertisement for "Roosevelt Rough Rider Mr. Mason Mitchell" on Sunday, August 13, 1899, *Syracuse Post Standard,* **Syracuse Public Library microfilm collection.**

He recounted in thrilling detail the storming of San Juan Hill in Cuba, bringing cheers and hearty applause from a large and enthusiastic crowd. To illustrate his talk, "a large number of views of the war were shown by stereopticon."[14] Mr. Mitchell, a native of Syracuse, made the point that, "the equipment of the National Guard was not up to the standard of that of the European armies."[15] The Spanish soldiers employed Mauser rifles, which used smokeless powder, capable of killing at a range of 3,000 yards, while the Americans were equipped with the

8.11 Advertisement for "The Most Novel Wedding of the Century," at the Lakeside Rustic Theater on Sunday, July 23, *Syracuse Post Standard*, July 23, 1899, Syracuse Public Library microfilm collection.

Springfield rifle that used black powder and only had a range of 1,000 yards. "The Spanish soldiers were able to kill before the American soldiers could get within range, and also that, owing to the fact that they used smokeless powder, it was almost impossible to locate them."[16] The following advertisement proclaims that Mr. Mason Mitchell of the Roosevelt Rough Riders will only give his talk on Sunday, August 13, 1899. Also, it gives information on the vaudeville novelty that will perform all the following week.

One of the more unusual, and perhaps bizarre, spectacles at the Lakeside Rustic Theater was the public marriage of Mr. Berta Marion Smith to Miss Lillian Easterbrook on Sunday, July 23, 1899. The illustration below is the advertisement for the wedding, open to all who purchased round-trip tickets on the Syracuse, Lakeside and Baldwinsville Railroad.

This was a sensationalized event, not unlike the "Who Wants to Marry a Millionaire" television program that aired early in the twenty-first century. An estimated fifteen thousand people came by streetcars, boats, carriages, and bicycles to witness the ceremony. A special detail of 'bluecoats' was hired to keep order and prevent pickpocketing. The bridal trolley car arrived by 4:30 PM, decked out in white bunting and streamers from top to bottom. The bride arrived wearing her travel attire and spent an hour changing into her wedding gown in one of the theater's dressing rooms. The bride's white satin gown was trimmed with chiffon lace, pearls and diamonds, and she carried a bouquet of roses. The large crowd grew impatient, chanting repeatedly for the fun to begin. The newspapers reported that, "one wag quipped, 'I hope she can get breakfast quicker than she can dress,' before being silenced by his wife."[17]

In a few minutes the short Episcopal service was over, and the newlyweds marched from the stage in a procession. "The groom took the bride by the arm and escorted her portly form away, and the crowd went home with their curiosity satisfied."[18] The bridal party had a wedding feast at the Maple Bay Hotel, and later the bride and groom were driven to the Yates Hotel, where a *Post Standard* reporter was eager for an interview only a half-hour after their arrival. The groom said, "I am more than satisfied with the way things went off. . . . The Lakeside Road gave us $50.00 in cash."[19]

It's hard to say who got more out of this, the newlyweds who received lavish publicity, or the trolley company who sold thousands of tickets and more than recouped their fifty dollar wedding gift investment. One can only hope the Smiths' marriage lasted longer than the one in the recent television spectacle!

In addition to a large hotel, Maple Bay/Lakeside Park also provided spots for tenting and small story-and-a-half summer cottages. This offered an alternate form of escape from the heat and busy streets of Syracuse. The summer residents were enticed to come to Lakeside Park because of its excellent streetcar connection and because every camper could experience his own idea of amusement. Such things as frequent clambakes, performances at the Rustic Theater, dancing, bowling, shooting, rowing, swimming, and just sitting around the campfire with friends, were all offered at Lakeside Park.

An August 1899 article in the *Syracuse Post Standard* describes how many Syracusans were enjoying themselves at their little cottages. Inside their canvas tent,

8.12 Postcard of tollgate at entrance to the Boulevard, Syracuse, N.Y., postmark 1909, published by William Judd, Syracuse, N.Y. and Leipzig, made in Germany, collection of the author.

"Camp Merry Makers," the Charles Wilkin family seemed to have everything necessary for summer comfort. "Last Wednesday evening Mr. Wilkin entertained a number of his friends with an old-fashioned campfire. His camp was brilliantly illuminated for the occasion with Japanese lanterns, and there was a pyrotechnic display."[20]

The Gradual Decline of Maple Bay/Lakeside Park

"The King of All Summer Resorts" continued to promote large outings to the amusement resort, and a variety of contests were planned to entertain the crowds. "The exhibitionists [acrobats] made a butter-fly leap into the lake from a high tower. Bicycle races to the tollgate at Hiawatha Road and back [on State Fair Boulevard] were participated in by various ages. Across the tracks where more space permitted, Melvin and Melvin ran a large pony ride concession"[21] The preceding old postcard is a view of the tollgate at the end of State Fair Boulevard where the bicycle races ended. Perhaps the stagecoach, surrey, and early automobile are returning from an outing to Lakeside Park.

Even during the early days of Maple Bay, the resort was not immune to trouble caused by 'toughs.' One night in early October, 1895, just before the trolley line reached Maple Bay, a group of six bullies from neighboring communities entered Mike Gafney's saloon at Maple Bay and refused to pay for their drinks after the second round. Because Mr. Gafney did not have the manpower to collect the money, the group of six left without paying and journeyed by surrey to Pleasant Beach, where they planned to try the same trick. "In the meantime, Gafney, riding a fast horse, hurried to Pleasant Beach. Here Mike and his friends, old man Hecker and his sons, Sully, Joe, and John, prepared a warm reception for the chiselers."[22]

The six men ordered a second round of drinks before paying for the first round, as they had at Maple Bay, but when they stated that they didn't intend to pay for them, out came a group of men armed with bung-starters, a wooden hammer used to remove bungs from beer barrels, and in thirty seconds the punks were overcome. They were tossed into a lumber wagon and brought to the tollgate at the end of the Boulevard, ending up sleeping the night off in the Solvay jail.

Many of the Onondaga Lake resorts hired special policemen, called bluecoats, who reported to the county sheriff any cases of pickpocketing or fights. A June 1899 article mentions three cases of people having their pockets picked for what today would be considered trivial amounts of money. The article mentions that the police have been watching for, "a young man who usually wears a black derby hat and a gray suit. It is said that he has been operating for some time at surrounding resorts and knows his business to a dot. He can get into a crowd and get out again without being observed, and invariably carries away something of value to him."[23]

In 1905, Lakeside Park was opened on May 28, for the summer season, featuring an enlargement to the dancing pavilion. The proprietors, the Corrollo brothers, claimed to have spent ten thousand dollars on improvements and proclaimed the dance floor to be the largest in the state outside of Coney Island. Also featured were pony rides for children and an electric theater that showed moving pictures all day. On July 10, the fifty member German Marine Band performed to a good-sized audience. In a newspaper interview by the *Syracuse Post Standard*, Conductor Herr Louis

Kidermann explained how the musicians were picked from various ships of the German navy and currently were on tour of the United States. The reporter mentioned Herr Kindermann spoke English well but never drinks beer.

Also during the first decade of the twentieth century, boxing matches were held at Maple Bay. In one of these prize fights, a local pugilist, or boxer, from Syracuse was fatally injured in a bare-fisted contest. This unfortunate event became a blemish on the resort's reputation as a family-oriented place, causing many to avoid it. During its last years, local gangs from the North Side and Tipperary Hill sections of Syracuse, Liverpool, Baldwinsville, and Solvay used Maple Bay as a site to settle turf wars, with numerous bloody fights becoming a common occurrence.

8.13 Maple Bay, 2000, photo by author.

In relatively short order the buildings became rundown and shabby, and the hotel was the last active remnant of the resort. Bill Ryan, the last operator of the hotel, finally had it demolished. Thus, the Lakeside resort slipped quietly into oblivion, without any sign of its former glory remaining today. However, anyone driving along State Fair Boulevard near the P & C Warehouse can look for Lakeside Road, and can see where this King of Resorts once reigned.

This photo, taken in the fall of 2000, is a good example of why so many Central New Yorkers today find it hard to believe the west shore of Onondaga Lake once bustled with resorts. This tranquil spot, where Maple Bay/Lakeside Park was located, provides an idyllic place for kayaking or walking along the tree-lined trail, but no hint of what was once there.

Notes

1. "Maple Bay," *Baldwinsville Gazette*, 20 August 1891.

2. "A Lakeside Feast," *Syracuse Standard*, 5 September 1890.

3. "Moonlight On The Lake," *Syracuse Journal*, 21 September 1891.

4. "For Outdoor Sports," *Syracuse Standard*, 8 August 1890.

5. "An Open Air Theater," *Syracuse Post Standard*, 12 June 1899.

6. "Band Concert Today," *Syracuse Post Standard,* 9 July 1899.

7. "Music and Living Pictures," *Syracuse Post Standard,* 19 August 1899.

8. "The Town Goes to See Fireworks," *Syracuse Journal,* 15 July 1899.

9. "Thousands Crowded to See Fireworks," *Syracuse Standard,* 15 July 1899.

10. "Thousands Crowded to See Fireworks."

11. "No Submarine Bombs in the Lakeside Display," *Syracuse Post Standard,* 5 August 1899.

12. "No Submarine Bombs in the Lakeside Display."

13. A. J. Christopher, "Sketches of Yesterday, Maple Bay or Lakeside Park, "*Baldwinsville Messenger,* 12 April 1962.

14. "Should Be Better Equipped," *Syracuse Post Standard,* 14 August 1899.

15. "Should Be Better Equipped."

16. "Should Be Better Equipped."

17. "Miss Easterbrook and Mr. Smith Were Married at Maple Bay," *Syracuse Post Standard,* 24 July 1899.

18. "Miss Easterbrook and Mr. Smith Were Married at Maple Bay."

19. "Miss Easterbrook and Mr. Smith Were Married at Maple Bay."

20. "Camping On Onondaga," *Syracuse Post Standard,* 20 August 1899.

21. "Camping On Onondaga."

22. A. J. Christopher, "Sketches of Yesterday, The Six Toughs," *North Syracuse Star News,* 22 September 1960.

23. "Sneak Thieves Get in Work at Lake Resorts," *Syracuse Post Standard,* 26 June 1899.

CHAPTER 9
THE MAURERS' LONG BRANCH RESORT, 1882-1938

The Long Branch Amusement Park was the creation of Ben and George Maurer, two immigrants who arrived from Germany when they were young children. As residents of Liverpool, New York, they grew up and found jobs in the local salt industry putting together barrels for salt, among other jobs. In 1882, they purchased land just north of Maple Bay next to the Onondaga Lake outlet. At that time, large groves of American chestnut trees grew in this area, so the park received its name from the long branches of this majestic tree. Due to the blight in 1915, these trees are no longer in existence.

A June 16, 1884, *Syracuse Standard* article mentions that, "the firm of Maurer and Company consisting of George and B. Maurer and Frederick C. Shug have recently purchased this grove and have begun work towards erecting a permanent two-story building."[1] It goes on to explain that the site selected for the building was a portion of a circular mound about twelve or fourteen feet in diameter which rises conspicuously in the grove. When digging the cellar, workers "came upon ten or twelve well-preserved skeletons, all arranged in order side by side, with their heads toward the south. Also found were arrowheads made of grey flint, but one is of pure white flint, about three inches in length, and was probably brought from the west."[2] The article concludes, "the work is still going on under the superintendence of Mr. Shug, who is very friendly and willing to show his discoveries to all visitors."[3] In an interview with James Duerr, formerly of Liverpool, he said that this same circular mound was located in the region where the parking lot is located today. He does not recall just when the mound was removed but thinks it was used for fill around Onondaga Lake to counteract the constant problem of erosion. When Kenneth Lang, an elderly resident of Liverpool, New York, was interviewed, he also remembered the mound on the present-day parking lot and a two-story building on top of this mound that was later moved down the Seneca River past Cold Springs, beyond where oil tanks are located today.

Traveling to Long Branch Park

In the late 1880s, Long Branch was becoming a favorite place to go for family or group outings by way of steamboat across Onondaga Lake. A May 1887 article in the *Syracuse Courier* announced that the grand opening of the 1887 season would be Sunday, May 29, and that, "a steamboat will leave the packet dock [on the Erie Canal] on Clinton Square for 'the Branch' in the morning, and boats will leave the Salina pier every hour. There will be a grand open-air concert during the day and other attractions."[4] The article also stated the recently built elegant steamer, *James Buchanan*, would make regular trips throughout the season, and that its boiler had been tested and approved by the government to assure passengers of the utmost safety.

By 1890, the People's Railway Company opened the Iron Pier Resort on the south shore of Onondaga Lake, near the end of Salina Street. At this point Syracusans would transfer from trolley or railroad to steamboat and travel to Long Branch on the opposite end of the lake. At Long Branch's height of popularity, steamboats departed the Iron Pier every half hour, but during this same time period the Syracuse, Lakeside and Baldwinsville trolley line was extended to reach the entrance of Long Branch Park as well, so people could travel by boat or trolley. People from Syracuse would continue to take steamboat outings on Onondaga Lake for many years, but the Iron Pier Resort was torn down in 1907, after nineteen years of existence, as other competing resorts were built along the west shore of Onondaga Lake.

When Long Branch Park was built in the 1880s, the residents of Syracuse would go to local recreational spots such as municipal swimming pools, zoos, or privately operated amusement parks. The motorcar was just being invented and not yet in widespread use, so people living in urban centers could not travel easily to the Adirondack Mountains or the Thousand Islands in a few hours like people today. In addition, many employees worked six days a week, so they did not have the leisure time for longer vacations. In the 1890s, on their days off, people could board an open-air trolley from the depot on Clinton Square, where the Syracuse Newspaper building is located today, and head for the lake resorts. At that time, the Onondaga County Courthouse and the Empire Hotel were located on the north side of Clinton Square, as shown in this old postcard depicting a bird's-eye view of Syracuse.

Clinton Square was the place where Syracusans started their excursions to Onondaga Lake Resorts. First they went by packet boat up the Oswego Canal,

9.1 **Bird's-eye view looking north, Syracuse, N.Y. Rudolph Bros., publisher, Syracuse, N.Y., made in Germany, no date, author's collection.**

Electric Terminal R. R. Station and Empire House,
Syracuse, N. Y.

9.2 Electric Terminal Railroad Station, Syracuse, N.Y., William Jubb, publisher, Syracuse, N.Y., post-mark date 1913, author's collection.

which ran along the east shore, to the 'Mud Lock' next to Long Branch, and then in 1899, the trolley took passengers along the west shore all the way to Long Branch in a fraction of the time it took to go by canal. The Electric Railway Terminal station was located on the corner of Salina and West Genesee Street.

In an article in the *North Syracuse Star News* on May 20, 1981, Joseph Wentworth stated that, "the resort [Long Branch] really came into its own in 1899 when the two-and-a-half-year-old Syracuse, Lakeside and Baldwinsville Trolley brought a railroad spur from the DL&W and extended its line from Maple Bay north to the entrance where a loop was extended to the park."[5] Due to this direct trolley line with Syracuse, on Sundays and during major summer holidays such as the Fourth of July, people could reach Long Branch Park in a few minutes. A round-trip ticket cost only twenty cents at the Electric Railway Terminal on Clinton Square. The following advertisements for Long Branch Park, which appeared in the *Syracuse Post Standard* on June 21, 1913, gives a clear idea of the Maurer family's dedication to a long heritage of service and constant improvements to the park.

When Helen Busher, age ninety in 1999, was asked what she remembered first about Long Branch Park, she stated, "the trolley ride to have a family picnic at Long Branch in 1916, when I was seven years old. These rides continued every summer until I was twelve. Often my family would accompany friends or join a church group for these outings. During the early 1920s, my father got a car, and the family began traveling to Fair Haven on Lake Ontario or the Thousand Islands to spend leisure time."[6] She went on to explain that, "my mother would pack a lunch of sandwiches, cookies, and milk that she kept in a cooler. My mother would bring a blanket to spread on the ground, and the grass all around was filled with thousands of wild violets."[7]

When Eugene Lee was interviewed in January 2000, at age 100, he remembered the giant American chestnut trees throughout Long Branch Park and how delicious the nuts were after roasting or boiling. "When I was about seven years

- 30th Season Under Same Management

LONG BRANCH PARK

Foot of Onondaga Lake.

The oldest and most reliable resort of Central New York, opens again with every facility for entertaining church, lodge or club picnics.

SOME OF THE ATTRACTIONS

Largest Dancing Pavilion in Central New York.	Carroussel.
	Barn Accommodations.
	New Row Boat Livery.
Six Up-to-date Brunswick-Balke Bowling Alleys.	Russian Toboggan.
	Photo Gallery.
	66 ft. Ferris Wheel.
Gasoline Launches for Rent.	Ariel Swing.
	Base Ball Grounds.
	American Box Ball Alley.
Hippodrome.	Miniature Lake.
Restaurant.	Circle Wave.
Shooting Gallery.	

Consult B. Maurer & Co. for Picnics.
Long Branch, N. Y.
Both Phones.

9.3 *Syracuse Post Standard* advertisements for Long Branch Park, June 21, 1913, Syracuse Public Library microfilm collection.

old, I remember getting a steamboat at the Iron Pier and going across Onondaga Lake, past Long Branch Park, through the outlet and on to the Three Rivers Resort at the convergence of the Seneca, Oneida, and Oswego Rivers."[8] When shown a picture of the *Eugene Petit* sternwheeler steamer taking passengers from Liverpool to Long Branch on the Oswego Canal, he stated that he was named Eugene after Mr. Petit. The steamer would be filled to capacity taking people to

9.4 The *Eugene Petit* steamer on the Oswego Canal, *Syracuse Sunday Post Standard*, December 19, 1943, Liverpool, New York Library's Crawford Collection.

Long Branch Park on the weekends, and the rest of the week it would haul cargo and people to Fulton on the Oswego Canal. In this picture of the *Eugene Petit* passengers are on their way to Long Branch with some evidently planning to take a bike ride. The steamer is passing a salt block along the Oswego Canal.

In a 1976 *Syracuse Herald American* newspaper article by Arlene Larue, the author remembered how her family and others would laugh and sing en route to the Onondaga Lake resorts. When they passed the Solvay Process sludge dump on the trolley they would sing, "Solvay Dump, Solvay Dump, you can tell when you're there by the smell in the air."[9] This little ditty helps to illustrate that during the very time of the "Golden Age of the Onondaga Lake Resorts," just before and after 1900, heavy industries were making their mark on the west shore of Onondaga Lake. The result of this collision course between leisure and business interests was the end of the lake resorts that were so much part of a way of life in Central New York 100 years ago.

9.5 Close-up of old carousel at Long Branch Park, Onondaga County Parks, Office of Museums.

What To Do Once at 'the Branch'

After arriving at Long Branch Park, many families would eat their picnic lunch which they prepared at home and brought to the park. Then they would seek out the rides on which they would spend their meager recreational funds. During the early years of Long Branch Park, the merry-go-round and roller coaster were located on the flat land next to the Onondaga Lake Outlet. After continued problems with severe spring flooding, the rides, pictured in this 1910 postcard, were moved away from the outlet to avoid the damage caused by flooding.

During its half-century existence, Long Branch Park has had several merry-go-rounds or carousels. Shown in the 1910 postcard, and also in the close-up of people riding the carousel, the carousels were an earlier version of the more famous carousel now found at the Carousel Mall, located in Syracuse, New York. The last

9.6 Scene of Long Branch Park, Syracuse, N.Y., Rudolph Brothers Manufacturers, Syracuse, N.Y., postmarked 1911, author's collection.

9.7 Spring flooding at Long Branch, early 1900s photograph, Onondaga County Parks, Office of Museums.

carousel at Long Branch is the one that is currently the showpiece of the shopping center. The Philadelphia Toboggan Company in Germantown, Pennsylvania, first built this carousel in 1909. It was brought to Long Branch Park in 1926, after first providing rides at amusement parks in Louisville, Kentucky; Worcester, Massachusetts; and Erie, Pennsylvania. The carousel stayed at Long Branch Park for fifteen years, until it was sold in 1941 to Roseland Park in Canandaigua, New York. For the next forty-three years, the carousel remained at Roseland Park, until it was sold in 1985 to the Syracuse-based Pyramid Construction Company for a record $397,500. Prior to this sale, it appeared the carousel might be divided up with various parts going to the highest bidder. The Pyramid Constitution Company kept the mechanized Wurlitzer organ intact, along with the hand-carved horses. Today a new generation of children and adults can enjoy this historic carousel that has made quite a journey over its lifetime of almost 100 years.

The merry-go-round has proven to be one of the most popular rides, possibly because it appeals to all ages and it is probably the ride that is least upsetting to the stomach! Eugene Lee mentioned that if you could catch the brass ring you would win a free ride on the carousel. He claimed he would, "always ride the horse on the outside of the carousel to get the brass ring."[10]

Besides the carousel, "the Branch" had a variety of other amusement rides. Over the years it had several different roller coasters. The earliest version of the

9.8 Workers on early roller coaster, Liverpool, New York Library's Crawford Collection.

roller coaster was the switchback railway designed in 1884 by L. A. Thompson for Coney Island. Riders would climb a long stairway to the top of a tower and enter a car that would descend on tracks, being propelled by gravity over a series of gentle rolling hills.

The coaster pictured with workers on top of the second level, was the Figure Eight coaster that the famous Philadelphia Toboggan Company, manufacturers of the carousel, first built in 1904. This roller coaster, unlike the switchback, had chains that pulled the cars to the highest hill, so riders did not have to get out of this new gravity ride before reaching the top of the highest hill. As time went on, improvements were added, such as a brake system in which a series of three sets of wheels locked cars to the track, and a safety bar kept riders in their seats throughout the ride. Ben Maurer's grandson, Kermit Maurer, remembers that before the roller coaster was opened up to the public each day, the Crouse brothers would look over the entire operation , tightening up bolts where needed. Then the empty cars were sent over the tracks in tandem to make sure everything was safe.

By 1928, Long Branch Park had added a roller coaster thriller called the Wild Cat. This three-fourths of a mile ride featured many curves taken at lightning speeds, starting with a ninety-foot breathtaking incline and rapid descent at the beginning of the ride. Between 1926 and 1930, Herbert Schmeck of the Philadelphia Toboggan Company designed thirty-eight such coasters, many of them called the Wild Cat or Comet. After the initial plunge from the highest incline, as the cars went over the next relatively steep second hill, the riders experienced the effects of temporary weightlessness for a few moments. After this ride, patrons would walk away on wobbly legs, exhilarated, but also often a bit queasy!

Another ride that was popular at 'the Branch' from the 1920s until its close in the late 1930s, was the Lindy Loop, named after Charles Lindberg's successful transatlantic flight. Two riders would travel in circular cars on tracks around a

9.9 Aerial swing Long Branch Park, collection of Todd Weseloh.

large circle, with the tracks going up and down. Inside the circular car, passengers swung back and forth and, at different points, made a full rotation inside their car, providing an exciting ride.

At various times Long Branch had bumper cars, or dodge-ems powered by electricity. These were popular with both young and old. Many people still enjoy this ride at fairs and carnivals today.

In 1913, for its thirtieth season, Long Branch advertised a sixty-six-foot Ferris wheel, a Russian toboggan and an aerial swing. One of the more interesting rides at 'the Branch' was the aerial swing that never seemed to go out of style from its introduction in 1902. During the first decade of the 1900s, passengers "rode in wicker gondolas similar to those found under a dirigible."[11] The huge tower from which the gondolas were suspended remained, but in 1927, the aerial swing was renamed the airplane. The wicker gondolas were replaced with deluxe cars resembling planes. Like the Lindy Loop, this was in honor of Charles Lindberg's famous 1927 transatlantic crossing, which stimulated a national fascination with the airplane. Possibly, if Long Branch Park had continued a little longer, chrome rocket ships would have replaced the airplanes, as they did in other amusement parks. Starting as early as the 1930s the technological fantasies of Buck Rogers and Flash Gordon stimulated an interest in space travel that has not lessened to the present.

Before it closed, 'the Branch' boasted of a real sight-seeing miniature railroad along the water and an Old Mill Chute that was advertised as the largest in New York State. This ride was similar to the Shoot-the-Chutes ride at White City, which took thrill seekers seated in boats down a long chute, landing suddenly in the water below. The Mill Chute was another successful patent of the Philadelphia Toboggan Company. It featured a darkened tunnel through which boats carrying up to six passengers glided down a thirty-five foot-ramp into the water below. This ride was especially popular with young couples, as it was similar to the Tunnel of Love rides of modern amusement parks. Kenneth Lang recalled taking young ladies on this ride, and he and a friend hit upon a scheme to prolong the romantic interlude in the darkened tunnel. The two young men would pocket an ice pick prior to embarking, and before the ride ended they would poke their ice picks into the wooden sides of the tunnel, creating their own braking system for the boat. When the ride operator noticed the delay, he pounded on the side of the tunnel to get them to move on.

If rides weren't someone's idea of a good time, he or she could patronize games of chance, a shooting gallery, a penny arcade, a photo gallery, a dance hall, or a bowling alley. Along the midways were booths where one could play various games of chance to win a kewpie doll or a cuddly teddy bear, made popular by President Teddy Roosevelt. In the 1895 photo, one of the owners of 'the Branch,' Ben Maurer, is about to attempt to knock down one of the dolls on the shelves in the back of the booth. This picture provides a glimpse of the styles popular at the turn of the twentieth century and how these games of chance could be easily modified to reflect whatever was popular at the moment. The large dance hall was used for roller-skating every afternoon and evening and for dancing on Saturday and Sunday evenings, to satisfy the largest number of interests.

The Maurer brothers also tried to satisfy seasonal interests. They put on a dramatic fireworks display on the Fourth of July. Rowboats were available during the

9.10 Ben Maurer in front of a game of chance on midway, 1895, Onondaga Historical Association.

summer, and in the winter one could go ice boating or have ice skating parties at Long Branch. The Maurers provided several baseball diamonds, and for a while had a semipro baseball team that would play area teams in a league.

As shown in these two postcards, the entrance gate to Long Branch Park changed several times over its half-century of existence. From 1899 until 1930, the trolley brought people to the entrance of Long Branch, where the tracks looped and a station was built. In the 1910 postcard, the entrance gate was very simple and groves of chestnut, oak, and maple provided a majestic sight as one walked up the

9.11 Entrance to Long Branch Park, Syracuse, N.Y., Rudolph Brothers Manufacturers, Syracuse, N.Y., postmarked 1910, author's collection.

9.12 The New Long Branch Park entrance arch, 1925, Onondaga County Parks, Office of Museums.

hill, to the top of the mound, where the dance pavilion and saloon were located. By the 1920s, the Long Branch welcome sign proclaimed a "New Long Branch Park – Let All Who Enter Here Leave Care Behind." This new entrance was built after the devastating tornado of 1912, which destroyed up to ninety percent of the trees at Long Branch. It was during the 1920s that the Maurers tried to revitalize Long Branch Park with new rides on the midway, but by the end of the decade trolleys no longer traveled to Long Branch from the city, and more and more people were using cars to go farther away from Syracuse for leisure activities.

Group Picnics and Lasting Social Contacts

From its beginning, and continuing today as part of the Onondaga County Park System, Long Branch has always been a popular picnic spot for families and organizations. 'The Branch' catered to annual summer picnics for such groups as the Farmer's Grange, political gatherings, church groups, and high school and college reunions. Helen Busher, a North Syracuse, New York resident, told how her parents first met at an annual farmers' picnic. The farmers' picnic would bring a crowd of over a thousand, and it was an event looked forward to for weeks. Each year the baby contest was a highlight. The best-looking baby under three years old could win a twenty dollar gold piece. A 1927 *Syracuse Newspaper* article mentioned that prizes were given for the largest family present, but it was noted that large families of eleven or more were not as common as a few years before. The article concludes that, "there were no horses and buggies there but large expensive cars which would shame many cars owned by city people. The customary baseball game was lacking, because it took all of the baseball diamonds and more, for parking spaces for the farmers' cars."[12] The postcard that follows shows the large crowd of eager mothers who brought their young children every Tuesday to Kiddies Day, a promotion to increase attendance during the week at Long Branch Park. George Mulligan remembered that as a child he'd scramble for the pennies and salt water taffy that the proprietor of Long Branch, Ben Maurer, would throw out on the grass for the kids at a certain time in the afternoon.

This 1915 view of a small band marching through Long Branch Park during a farmers' picnic, gives a good idea of this event's popularity with area farmers. The children in the foreground are enjoying the music as the band marches by. Note the abundance of parasols to shade parade goers in the hot sun. Likely, the band was playing a popular Sousa march.

Every Saturday morning during the first decade of the twentieth century, the *Syracuse Post Standard* would feature a section on leisure, vacation, and travel. This

9.13 Kiddies Day at New Long Branch Park, postcard by Curt Teich and Company, Chicago, no postmark, author's collection.

9.14 Ben Maurer leading band at Farmers' Picnic at Long Branch, August 19, 1915, Onondaga Historical Association archives.

section would also include weekly events, such as planned annual picnics. A July 11, 1914, article announced, "The Lutheran Church of Atonement will hold its outing at Long Branch Tuesday, having arranged with the Empire United Railways for a large amount of special service from this city."[13] That same day the Congregational Church from Oswego was holding its outing and, "Thursday will be Scotch Day at Long Branch on the occasion of the Syracuse Caledonian Club picnic. On Saturday the employees of the H.H. Franklin Manufacturing Company will hold their annual excursion at Long Branch."[14] This last picnic was attended annually by up to 5,000 people.

One of the oldest buildings at Long Branch Park was the building containing the dance hall and bowling alleys. This was a two-story building that was built into the side of a hill, so that picnic goers could walk into the dance hall from the top of the hill or into the bowling alley from the base of the hill. The 1910 Sanborn map of Long Branch Park shows this dual-purpose building at the bottom of the map between the roller coaster on the right and the carousel on the far left. After 1910, the Figure Eight roller coaster was demolished because of the annual spring floods along the Onondaga Lake Outlet. In the 1931 map, the latest roller coaster, the Wild Cat, is shown alongside other rides farther away from the Seneca River.

In the middle of Long Branch Park was a shady grove of trees with benches to rest on, neatly arranged flower gardens, and picket fences. The building housing the dance hall and downstairs bowling alley can be seen on the left, and the banner on the right is for the July picnic of the National Protective Legion. Passengers are leaving the trolley platform on the left and are entering the grove through the turnstiles. A couple of boys wearing knickers, in the center of this picture, seem anxious to get to the amusement rides.

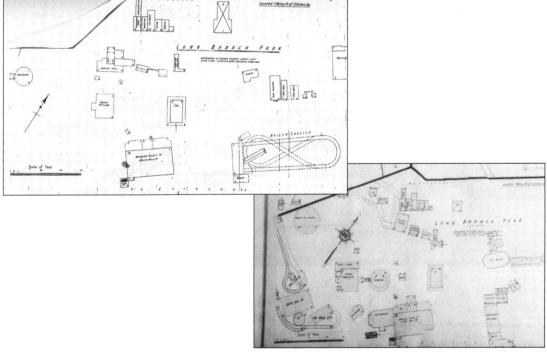

9.15 Sanborn map of Long Branch Park, 1910 and 1931, Onondaga Public Library microfilm collection, and Syracuse University Bird Library.

This June 18, 1910, picture shows the trolley turnstiles from the grove looking at the drumlin behind the tracks. For the return trip to Syracuse, passengers are told to take the trolley at the depot. It is interesting to compare the picture taken in 1910 with that taken after the tornado struck Long Branch Park in 1912. The fine American chestnut and oak trees are shattered with debris everywhere. The

9.16 The grove at Long Branch Park, collection of Todd Weseloh.

'Take Cars at Depot' sign is hanging by one end as onlookers survey the extensive damage.As time went on, the configuration of the midways and attractions at Long Branch would change, but the dance hall, with six bowling alleys and billiard tables on the first floor, would remain as a focal point until the park closed in 1938. This 1930s picture advertises a game of billiards or bowling for just fifteen cents. The upper portion of the roller coaster called the 'Wild Cat,' introduced to the park in the 1920s, can be seen in the background.

Like most Onondaga Lake resorts of the early-twentieth century, Long Branch had both a dance hall and an open-air dance pavilion for the summer months. During weekend evenings both young and old seemed to enjoy dancing to waltzes or popular dances, like the Charleston of the 1920s. During the early 1900s, single young people in their teens would meet on the dance floor on Saturday evenings, and eventually a kind of dance club was organized. A 1976 *Syracuse Herald American* article by Arlene Larue states that, "after an evening of dancing, the groups would see to it that each of the girls had a male escort to see her home."[15] Long Branch had special magic for Arlene Larue's parents because they were married two years after their first date, and they had first met at the Long Branch dance hall.

The 1910 Sanborn map of Long Branch shows a boathouse on the Seneca River outlet to Onondaga Lake. Here, rowboats were available for rent, and by 1920, Long Branch was advertising a new speedboat that could carry up to eight

9.17 Scene at Long Branch, June 18, 1910, collection of Todd Weseloh.

9.18 Sept. 17, 1912, picture of damage after tornado, no postmark, author's collection.

passengers and could travel at speeds up to forty miles per hour. This postcard illustrates people enjoying themselves in various watercrafts in the outlet. In the distance, people can be seen crossing the bridge that took visitors from the nearby Oswego Canal.

The Tornado of 1912

During a hot and muggy Sunday afternoon on September 15, 1912, a devastating tornado hit the northern suburbs of Syracuse. Particularly hard hit was

9.19 The dance hall and bowling alley building at Long Branch Park, Onondaga County Parks, Office of Museums.

9.20 The outlet at Long Branch Park, Syracuse, N.Y., Rudolph Brothers Manufacturers, Syracuse, N.Y., no postmark, author's collection.

Long Branch Park. It is believed that the storm formed near Cross Lake and struck Long Branch Park about 5:00 PM. Within minutes, the grove of chestnut trees was uprooted and snapped like pipe stems. After inflicting severe damage at Long Branch Park, the storm moved on to the Pitcher Hill area of North Syracuse and Collamer.

The extensive damage was described in a *Post Standard* article on September 16, reporting that, "the trolley station [at Long Branch] was demolished. The site upon which it stood was swept as though by a gigantic broom. . . . Approximately

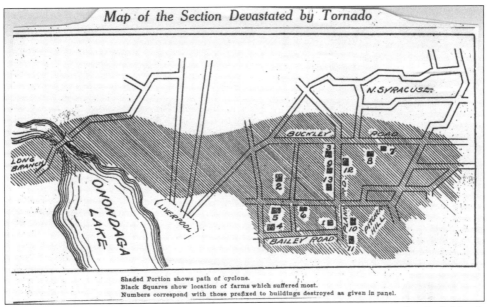

Map of the Section Devastated by Tornado

Shaded Portion shows path of cyclone.
Black Squares show location of farms which suffered most.
Numbers correspond with those prefixed to buildings destroyed as given in panel.

9.21 Map of the section devastated by tornado, front page of the *Syracuse Post Standard*, Monday morning, September 16, 1912. Syracuse Public Library microfilm collection.

three hundred people were at the resort, many of whom were at the station. William Madison, 53, who lived about three quarters of a mile from Long Branch, was instantly killed."[16] Madison and his wife had just arrived at Long Branch from Syracuse, and they were waiting for the rain to stop before walking home from the Long Branch station. The tornado demolished the station, and his body was found on the hillside about one hundred feet away. His wife suffered a broken arm and other serious injuries, but survived.

George Dopp, a motorman for the Syracuse, Lakeshore and Northern Railroad, was also killed when the tornado overturned his trolley at Long Branch Park. This 1912 postcard shows the site where George Dopp was killed when his trolley was blown over. The bowling alley building seems to have been spared major damage, but the severe damage to the large trees can be easily observed.

Bernie Maurer, the son of the owner, was playing billiards with family friend Norman Lee under the big dance hall when the storm hit. Maurer contained the people there so they would not run out among the fallen trees and dangerous electrical wires. During the height of the storm, Frank Phippen miraculously escaped death when his popcorn concession stand was picked up by the tornado and deposited upside down on the ground. Before the tornado arrived, about a hundred people were eating supper under the large pavilion on top of the hill. Within minutes the tornado had brought down the roof supports, trapping everyone underneath. Kermit Maurer recalls that when his father, Bernie Maurer, was told a hundred people were trapped, he got a fire axe to cut through the roof, expecting to find many dead. Instead, when he finally got through, he found all had survived with no major injuries. The roof had come down over the people like an umbrella, resting on the solid platform.

In the interview with 100-year-old Eugene Lee, he remembered observing the tornado from his home in Liverpool, when he was about thirteen years old.

9.22 Results of tornado at Long Branch, September 15, 1912, collection of Todd Weseloh.

"Immediately a friend and I rode our bikes down the towpath of the Oswego Canal, cut across to Willow Bay, and rode over the outlet bridge. We arrived at Long Branch within an hour after the tornado struck. I can remember the great destruction to the American chestnut trees, the same trees that had provided delicious nuts on prior visits to the park."[17]

Benjamin Maurer, who was sixty years old at the time, was stunned at the extent of damage to his park, but he stated that he would not give up yet and would rebuild. When he realized the extent of damage on that late summer Sunday afternoon, he arranged with city officials to have automobiles and carriages sent to Long Branch to take home hundreds of people who were stranded. The trolley line had been shut down due to so many fallen trees. To add further tragedy to this disaster, Mrs. Bernie Maurer, the daughter-in-law of the owner of Long Branch, died possibly of food poisoning from bad clams eaten at a family picnic at Long Branch. This added blow to Benjamin Maurer came within the week after the Sunday tornado. Oddly enough, Mrs. Bernie Maurer did not feel ill within twenty-four hours after eating the clams, as others had. She ran a high fever five days later and eventually died. Her mother, Mrs. Joseph Drais, "did not believe the clams caused her daughter's death,"[18] as reported in the September 20 *Syracuse Journal*.

Helen Busher told of her father and hundreds of other people going to see the destruction at Long Branch. Benjamin Maurer did rebuild the park after the severe destruction, and the park continued to be a popular recreation site on Onondaga Lake. In the May 31, 1913, edition of the *Syracuse Post Standard*, it was reported that Memorial Day was the official opening of Long Branch following the tornado destruction of September 1912. "The Empire United Railways has erected a new station in place of the one carried away by the tornado. Over 7,000 people from Syracuse and vicinity visited the Branch yesterday. Two-car trains were run between Syracuse and the Branch all day under seven-minute headway."[19] In

1913, Long Branch Park had managed to survive into its thirtieth season under the same management, despite the destructive tornado the previous year. For families, 'the Branch' was still a favorite getaway from the routines of life, as well as church, social, or civic organizations.

One of the most interesting interviews conducted for this book was with Kermit Maurer, the grandson of Long Branch owner, Ben Maurer. Kermit Maurer was born in 1911, the year before the destructive tornado demolished most of Long Branch except for the building that contained the dance floor and bowling alleys. During his childhood, Kermit had the unique experience of actually living in the apartment above the dance floor during the summer months. This must have been the ultimate childhood dream, to spend one's summer vacation enjoying the rides, games, and food at Long Branch. "When I'd see the other kids leaving at the end of a day at Long Branch, I felt sorry that they had to leave for home on the trolley while the whole summer was ahead of me at the park," Kermit reminisced. "At the end of the day I went back to our apartment and was lulled to sleep by the music from the dance floor and the sounds of the various amusements."[20] Besides going on the rides and trying the shooting gallery whenever he wished, he could make his own sundaes at the soda fountain. This was situated next to the dance floor, and constructed so that it was accessible to both the dance floor and to patrons outside the pavilion. Also just inside the dance floor, as people walked in, was a large Wurlitzer organ that played all day long. During the evening, a small orchestra played in a balcony above the dance floor as patrons danced or sat listening to the music.

Kermit Maurer remembered that one of his favorite games was the pig shoot. The object of the game was to throw three balls through a hole in the canvas to trigger a paddle. This in turn opened one of numerous pens, each containing a small white pig. The released pig would run down the chute and eventually return to its cage to receive its reward of milk. Some contestants mistakenly tried to claim the pig for their prize, reaching over the counter to try to grab it, and had to be restrained. At the end of the summer the pigs had not grown much, in spite of being milkfed.

The prizes given out at Long Branch were interesting in themselves. At day's end people could be seen walking to the trolley carrying various wicker ware items, locally made in Liverpool. Indian blankets made by members of the Onandaga Nation were also popular as prizes. Sometimes when Ben Maurer would learn that a large family had only enough money left for the trolley fare home, he would pull out a few bills from the large wad of money he always carried and hand it to the head of the family.

In the early 1920s, when Kermit Maurer was growing up, there were no cash registers at the various games. To play, people just put their coins in a cigar box. Often at the end of the weekend there would be thousands of dollars kept in the living quarters above the bar room until the banks opened on Monday. In connection with taking the proceeds to the bank, Kermit recalled two stories. On one occasion the man assigned to take the money to be deposited was driving too fast, and the car rolled over three times, spewing thousands of bills all over. People materialized quickly upon the scene, which resembled an Easter egg hunt, as they scrambled to retrieve and keep the bills. On another occasion there had been a rash of robberies in the area, in which empty satchels were placed in the roadway to decoy unsuspecting motorists. Upon stopping to investigate, the curious but unlucky drivers and their passengers were set upon by the thieves and robbed. About this same period a deposit of $7,000 was being taken to the bank by Long Branch officials, with the money in a bag strapped to the car's running board. When they stopped to let off some park employees at Clinton Square, they realized the bag was missing. Upon retracing their route they discovered the bag, still containing the $7,000 untouched. Apparently people had become afraid to stop because of recent robberies.

During the end of the 1931 baseball season, Ben Maurer arranged for Lefty Grove and the Philadelphia Athletics team to come and play an exhibition game on the Long Branch diamond. Local All Stars played the World Champions, with Lefty Grove pitching the ninth inning. Kermit recalled, "The All Stars were allowed to send up their best batters, but Lefty struck out three batters in a row to end the game."[21]

The End of Long Branch

During the Roaring 20s, things changed. More and more families were able to purchase cars that could take them beyond the entertainment facilities on Onondaga Lake. At first, Long Branch Park and other Onondaga Lake resorts had to compete with Frenchman's Island and Sylvan Beach on Oneida Lake, and Lakeside Park on Owasco Lake. But as time went on more advertisements for excursions to the Adirondacks and the Thousand Island resorts appeared in the Saturday travel section of the Syracuse newspapers.

By 1930, the trolleys stopped running to Long Branch Park from Clinton Square in Syracuse, and in 1938 Long Branch Park closed forever. In that year, the park had been closed all season, and in August it was reported that the Onondaga County Sheriff's office was called to investigate the looting of metal. The country was in the depths of the Great Depression, and the Maurer family was unable to invest additional money to maintain and improve the park in the way it had been kept for fifty-five previous years. By 1938, the founder of Long Branch, Benjamin Maurer, had been dead for six years, and his son, Bernard Maurer, was ready to sell the ninety-six remaining acres of the park to Onondaga County, which was in the process of developing a park along the east shore of Onondaga Lake.

'The Branch' would be open one last time to area group gatherings. In the *Syracuse Post Standard* of August 24, 1938, it was reported that, "the resort will be taken over September 17 and 18, on one day by the Veterans of Foreign Wars and on the other by the Republican Club of Geddes."[22] By 1941, the carousel was sold to Roseland Park, and many of the remaining buildings were gradually lost when their roofs collapsed under the weight of heavy snow. In 1948, Long Branch again made the news when a fire leveled the old dance hall and bowling alley building. The days of Long Branch Park as the public playground for Central New York had passed into history. Eventually other amusement parks, such as Suburban Park, would rise in popularity, later to receive the same fate as Long Branch Park. Only old pictures of "the Branch" still remain to keep alive an understanding of what life was like along the shores of Onondaga Lake 100 years ago.

Notes

1. "A Mound of Graves," *Syracuse Standard*, 16 June 1884.

2. " A Mound of Graves."

3. " A Mound of Graves."

4. "Grand Opening at Long Branch," *Syracuse Courier*, 20 May 1887.

5. "As it was – Onondaga Lake: Long Branch," *North Syracuse Star News* 20 May 1981.

6. Helen Busher (age ninety), personal interview,November, 1999.

7. Helen Busher.

8. Eugene Lee (age 100), personal interview, January 2000.

9. Arlene Larue, "All Our Yesterdays, Magic and Mystery of Long Branch," *Syracuse Herald American*, 1 Feb 1976.

10. Eugene Lee, personal interview, January 2000.

11. *Euclid Beach Park Is Closed For the Season*, L. Bush, E. Chukeyne, R. Hehr, R. Hershey. Amusement Parks Books, Inc., Fairview Park, Ohio, 1977, p. 100.

12. "Old Timer Finds Farmers Picnic Has Changed Much" (from Onondaga Historical Association Files), *Syracuse Newspapers*, 1927.

13. "Holds Picnics on Onondaga Lake," *Syracuse Post Standard*, 11 July 1914.

14. "Holds Picnics on Onodaga Lake."

15. Arlene Larue, "All Our Yesterdays, Magic and Mystery of Long Branch."

16. "Long Branch Wrecked; Two Cars Demolished," *Syracuse Post Standard*, 16 September 1912.

17. Eugene Lee, (age 100), personal interview, January 2000.

18. "Mrs. Maurer, Poisoned By Clams, Is Dead." *Syracuse Journal*, 20 September 1912.

19. "Trolley Lines Take 22,000 Out of City," *Syracuse Post Standard*, 31 May 1913.

20. Kermit Maurer, personal interview, January, 2002.

21. Kermit Maurer.

22. "Park Closed After 55 Years," *Syracuse Post Standard*, 24 August 1938.

CHAPTER 10
PRISTINE PLAYGROUND TO CHEMICAL DISASTER
NEW PLANS FOR THE TWENTY-FIRST CENTURY

Recognizing The Lake's Recreational Value

"Our beautiful lake will present continuous villas ornamented with shady groves and hanging gardens and connected by a wide and splendid avenue that shall encircle its entire waters."

-From a speech by Harvey Baldwin, first mayor of Syracuse, in 1847.

It has been over 150 years since Harvey Baldwin first realized the recreational value of Onondaga Lake to the citizens of Syracuse. During the late nineteenth century and the first decade of the twentieth century, this dream was realized on the west shore of the lake, as the (State Fair) Boulevard was built along the lakeside and at least seven lake resorts were built to meet the recreational needs of Syracusans. At first trolley service only provided transportation to Salina Pier, Geddes Pier or the Iron Pier, where one would board a steamboat for a beautiful ride to one of the west shore resorts. As early as 1880, the Lackawanna Railroad constructed a railroad spur on the west shore of Onondaga Lake, later to be followed by a competing electric trolley line in the 1890s, both promoting the growth of recreational facilities along the west shore. In 1893, the 'Boulevard,' which stretched for six miles along the west shore, was built on refuse from the Solvay Process works, allowing access to the resorts by carriage.

During this same time period much of the east shore was marshland. The Oswego Canal, running along the east shoreline, was built in 1828 to facilitate the growth of the salt industry. Covering much of the land at the southern end of Onondaga Lake were hundreds of acres of solar salt sheds and salt blocks where salt brine was processed to produce salt crystals. One of the few entertainment spots on the eastern shore was the rowdy Mud Lock Tavern, located on the canal block between the Oswego Canal and the Seneca River. This 1895 photo shows the tavern with the turn-of-the-century owner's name emblazoned on the roof. The bar was on the first floor wing, with the kitchen and dining room located in the main structure; four bedrooms and a sitting room were on the second floor. The tavern and lock tender's shanty were demolished in 1933 when the Onondaga County Emergency Work Bureau restored the nearby Mud Lock.

During the nineteenth century many changes were made to Onondaga Lake. First, the lake was lowered two feet in 1822 by dynamiting a reef at the outlet to

10.1 The Mud Lock Tavern of Frank Wise, photographer unknown, 1895, Onondaga Co. Parks, Office of Museums.

Seneca River. Before this was done, the area where Hiawatha Boulevard and the Carousel Mall are today, was under water. Malaria was an ever-present concern as long as the swamps existed. By 1862, the salt industry had its peak year of production, producing nine million bushels of salt that year. Only four years later in 1866, the *Syracuse Journal* editor began a crusade to make Onondaga Lake available for the public's use and enjoyment and to rid the southern shoreline of the unsightly salt vats, many of which were built on reclaimed land. He stated, "We should like to see an army of enraged Syracusans march directly through the ugly salt vats and sweep everything before them for a space of 150 feet in width."[1]

After the Civil War, the increased competition from western sources of salt led to the long gradual decline of the salt industry that continued until the 1920s, when the last salt vat disappeared. By 1878, Salina Street was extended north to the Salina Pier, making the lake accessible by steamboat, and transportation to the southeast shore was improved.

The Seeds of Disaster

During the golden age of the west shore resorts, the seeds of their demise were being planted. In 1884, the Solvay Process Company began producing soda ash, and by 1885 the United States Fishing Commission reported, "fishing in Onondaga Lake dropped from 20,000 pounds to 1,000 pounds in just one year. In 1898 the tasty Onondaga Lake white fish, which had appeared on the menus of restaurants along the East Coast, disappeared entirely."[2]

During 1896, backyard privies were prohibited in the city of Syracuse, and sewers were built which flowed directly into Onondaga Creek, Harbor Brook, and eventually Onondaga Lake. This increased pollution of the lake led to a state ban in 1901 on ice cutting in Onondaga Lake because of impurities in the water. When the New York State Fair opened in 1890, one of its attractions was its fine view of Onondaga Lake. However when Solvay Process shifted its dumping from the southern end of the lake to the west shore, the piles of white soda ash waste became so high that by the 1920s the view of the lake became obstructed.

The following picture was taken between 1890 and 1910. The Solvay Process plant can be viewed in the foreground next to the Erie Canal, with open land between it and the west shore. The old Syracuse Yacht Club that burned down in 1917 can be seen on the left side of this photo. This flat farmland has now been developed and much of the shoreline is built up with waste from the Solvay Process Company.

10.2 Solvay Process Company, 1890-1900, Solvay Library archives.

What was the Solvay Process? The salt industry was a major employer for about one hundred years, but in 1884 the Solvay Process Company began production of soda ash. That industry would be a major employer for almost one hundred years. The company chose to locate in the rural town of Geddes because it commonly was believed that the source of the brine lay in a large salt deposit under the lake. And there was the availability of cheap transportation via canal and railroad. Another reason was the proximity of limestone quarries, a necessary ingredient for production. In 1879, local geologist William B. Cogswell learned of a European process for production of ammonia soda using large quantities of salt, limestone, and coal. He secured permission from the Ernest and Alfred Solvay Company of Belgium to make soda ash and received financial backing from Rowland Hazard to construct the factory in 1881. It was not until 1888 that Mr. Cogswell obtained brine of sufficient strength to make the process economical. He finally hit the salt bed at a depth of 1,216 feet in the area south of the city. The brine was pumped to the plant along Onondaga Lake. Soda ash, the end product, was used in producing rayon, plastics, glass, detergents, and explosives.

Unfortunately, large quantities of a white chalky waste compound of calcium carbonate and calcium hydroxide were produced, and this waste was first pumped directly into Onondaga Lake for many years until the company was threatened with criminal action by the State Attorney General in 1907. Beginning in 1907, the chalky waste was dumped along the west shoreline, and starting in 1920, it was mixed with Syracuse sewage sludge on land purchased by the city from the estate of Frank

Heberle, the former owner of Lake View Point Resort. Over a fifty-year period the waste beds eventually covered four hundred acres and reached a height of eighty feet, completely obstructing a view of the lake from the State Fairgrounds.

This waste accumulation increased the lake's salinity and led to the destruction of grassy feeding areas for various fish species along the shore. When Ken Wentworth was interviewed in 1985, he did not put all the blame on Solvay Process for the disappearance of the whitefish, however; he also blamed it on Syracuse sewage and the building of a railway. His father always claimed the fish disappeared, "the same year New York Central put the railway around the lake. In one place, near Hiawatha Boulevard, they had trouble with a sinkhole. Carload after carload of fill was poured into the sinkhole before they could get a roadbed to sustain the tracks. His father always believed that in the winter time the whitefish went up an underground river, up in the hills somewhere, and when they blocked it off, they didn't come back next spring."[3]

The 1892 and 1908 maps of Onondaga Lake's south shore illustrate that many acres of land were reclaimed by lowering the lake level and by filling with Solvay Process waste. The railway that Ken Wentworth spoke of is labeled "Syracuse Junction Railway," and in 1892 it went across a portion of the lake. By 1908 this railway had become part of the shoreline because so much land had been filled. On the 1892 map you can see the original course for Onondaga Creek, but by 1908, the old channel of Onondaga Creek has been filled. The Iron Pier Harbor is located at what used to be the mouth of the creek. The whitefish may not have gone in an underground river, but it seems likely their breeding grounds were permanently destroyed with all the fill put into Onondaga Creek.

Besides the Solvay Process calcium deposits located along the lakeshore, a large portion of the lake bottom is also covered with this waste. Today, "the top four (or more) feet of sediment is contaminated with mercury and other heavy

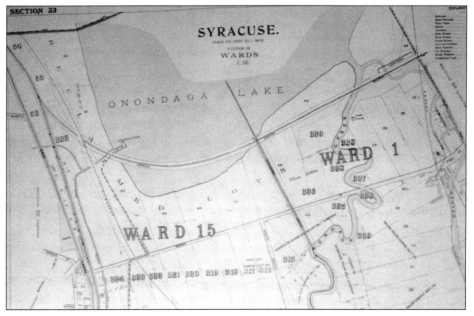

10.3 Syracuse, New York, Ward 1, Section 1, 1892 Atlas by Vose and Co., Onondaga Co. Parks, Office of Museums.

10.4 Syracuse, New York, Plate 31, 1908 Atlas by GM Hopkins Co., Philadelphia, PA, Onondaga Co. Parks, Office of Museums.

metals, PCBs, petroleum and other organic pollutants."[4] The Solvay Process Company, now Honeywell, Inc., is responsible for mercury contamination, a byproduct of the company's two chlorine-manufacturing plants. Other toxic substances that leaked or were discharged into the lake by the Solvay Process Company include benzene toluene, chlorinated benzenes used to make mothballs and polyaromatic hydrocarbons, a component of coal.

The Solvay Process Company Was Not the Only Polluter

The pollution of Onondaga Lake is not the responsibility of Solvay Process alone. Crucible Steel has dumped its chromium waste on a site just north of Lake View Point, and PCBs have migrated along Ley Creek, a tributary of Onondaga Lake, and in effect a chemical conduit from the GM Fisher Guide Plant just northeast of Syracuse. Bristol Laboratories (in DeWitt) added to this chemical stew with waste products from its penicillin plant. Syracuse China has disposed of broken dishes there. "In the 1950s, one estimate was that 139 industries used Onondaga Lake as their waste basin."[5]

The Metropolitan Sewage Treatment Plant on the south shore of Onondaga Lake has upgraded its facility several times during the 1970s and 1980s, but the lake continues to be plagued by high levels of ammonia and phosphorus discharge mainly from the sewage treatment plant. Both of these discharges have caused 'algae blooms' that consume large quantities of dissolved oxygen, which fish need to survive. Frequently, Onondaga Lake continues to receive a high degree of bacterial contamination when the antiquated sewage system overflows during rainy periods, sending raw sewage directly into the lake.

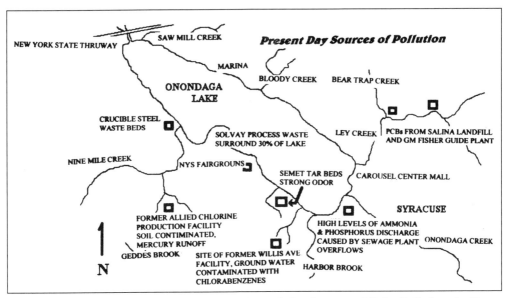

10.5 Map of the Tributaries of Onondaga Lake and the Sources of Lake Pollution, by Bryan Thompson.

What was the one event that awakened the public and politicians to what was happening to Onondaga Lake? The Thanksgiving Day disaster of 1943! While the residents of Lakeland slept, an eight-foot wall of goo from the Solvay Process Company waste beds was created when a retaining dike gave way. An area covering one square mile was inundated, including the State Fairgrounds, State Fair Boulevard, homes, and the DL&W Railroad tracks. When a guard returned to the air depot on the Fairgrounds about 3:00 AM, he found, "his station house floating towards him on the approaching wall of white waste. He turned to run but slipped and fell, losing his false teeth and revolver. Leaving both, he got up and ran from the oncoming waste which formed a moving billow more than eight feet high."[6]

Finally, An Organized Effort to Revive the Lake

In 1928, Joseph Griffin, secretary of the Onondaga Park and Regional Planning Board, formulated a plan that called for a park around the entire lake. This plan was not implemented until 1931 when the Onondaga County Work Relief Bureau began to construct a county park on the east shore of the lake, filling in the swampland and the abandoned Oswego Canal. Workers used a dredge to pump sludge from the bottom of the lake into the canal and swamp, planted thousands of trees and shrubs, rebuilt the Mud Lock, constructed the Salt Museum, the Ste. Marie Mission, Griffin Field, and a four-lane parkway for a total cost of $903,048. This local relief program employed over two thousand and became a model for President Franklin Roosevelt's WPA program. In the end, the work would fall short of Joseph Griffin's master plan for a park around the whole lake, but later politicians would take up this dream.

One of the more unusual make-work projects on the east shore of Onondaga Lake was the 700 by 150 foot Danforth Salt Swimming Lake that was constructed near the site where Asa Danforth and Comfort Tyler first made salt in 1788. It was

Crandall Melvin's suggestion that this salt-water bathing facility be named 'Danforth' after one of the earliest salt makers. In 1933, the salt lake was completed with the salt content being supplied by nearby salt springs. The people of greater Syracuse would enjoy this miniature salt lake into the early 1950s, and a portion of it still exists next to the Onondaga Lake Parkway just before reaching Route 81. This old picture shows young and old enjoying Danforth Salt Lake with its high degree of buoyancy at a time when pollution from the city sewage plant prevented bathing in the adjacent Onondaga Lake. In its first three months, over one hundred thousand people enjoyed this new recreational facility.

10.6 Danforth Salt Lake, Onondaga Co. Parks, Office of Museums.

During the mid-twentieth century the pollution of Onondaga Lake continued to worsen in spite of the 1943 Thanksgiving Day sludge spill. At one point during the 1946 campaign, Governor Thomas Dewey told members of the Onondaga Lake Reclamation Association, "No private corporation should be allowed to spoil a community asset."[7]

The governor talked of plans to remove tons of sludge along the shoreline so to extend the fairgrounds down to the shore of Onondaga Lake. After the election this plan was put on hold. It was not until 1953 that the State of New York agreed to drop its damage claims against Solvay Process/Allied Chemical caused during the 1943 sludge spill. In return for dropping its damage claim, the state received four hundred acres of waste beds to build State Fair parking lots and Route 690 along the west shore of the lake.

Syracuse newspapers in the early 1950s were full of articles envisioning the beautification of polluted Onondaga Lake. In a banner article, the January 14, 1951, *Syracuse Post Standard* stated, "In short, the natural beauty of the lake will be restored. Its waters will be clearer. Its recreational values will be doubled and tripled. It will be a treasure to the city and county, not an eyesore."[8]

Planners went ahead with construction of a 16,000-car parking facility on top of the Solvay waste beds in preparation for the 1954 State Fair, and construction on a five-and-a-half-mile expressway linking the State Thruway with Syracuse. The next part of the plan called for the recreational development of the eighty-foot high barren landscape formed by the Solvay alkali waste along the west shore. On Lake View Point planners included such facilities as a golf course, various sports fields and an aqua-stadium along the shoreline. Replanted with grass and shrubs, Lake View Point would have been returned to a natural state that once drew pic-nickers in the 1870s.

The Onondaga County Park and Regional Planning Board developed a plan in 1955 calling for a west shore park on Onondaga Lake that would extend from Nine Mile Creek along the shore to the Barge Canal Terminal. Their plan includ-ed the construction of "a series of lagoons to be dredged behind the present shoreline, leaving a buffer of undeveloped natural cover between the lagoons and the arterial highway. The areas between the lagoons and the lake can be filled above yearly inundation levels with material excavated from the lagoons."[9] This plan would have made available parks along the west shore that would be largely immune from the springtime flooding that plagued most of the nineteenth cen-tury resorts. In the end, these plans for the recreational development of the west shore during the 1950s would be put off until a later date.

In the 1960s the Environmental Protection Agency established rigid standards regulating industrial waste deposits. Since 1968, a lake monitoring program has kept track of the improving water quality of the lake, in part the result of a new sewage treatment plant that was constructed in 1979. During the mid 1970s, an Onondaga Lake Environmental Action Plan was prepared for the Syracuse-Onondaga County Planning Agency, calling for the development of a trail system for cyclists, snowmobilers, and hikers, public amenities for recreationalists, and the placement of historical markers along the west shore noting the historic sig-nificance of the shoreline. The action plan, when completed would encompass trails around the entire lake. Like previous plans, these plans also would go unful-filled, but the idea of a trail around the entire lake would come alive again at the end of the twentieth century.

Back to the Future, "Loop the Lake"

Ever since 1847, when Syracuse's first mayor envisioned an avenue encircling Onondaga Lake with shady groves on either side, planners for over one hundred and fifty years have been trying to make this dream a reality. Because of increased public awareness of the pollution that still exists in the lake, this dream has a much better chance of seeing fulfillment as the citizens of the region realize the eco-nomic value of the lake's use as a year-round recreational site instead of an indus-trial and sewage dumping ground.

The latest "Loop the Lake" plan for recreational development is not new, but it is more comprehensive in meeting a wider variety of needs for cyclists, walkers, joggers, wheelchairs, and cross-country skiing. The twelve-mile route around the lake would, "access Carousel Center, the State Fairgrounds, the existing West Shore trail, the popular East Shore Recreational Trail and historic sites at

Onondaga Park, and the P & C Stadium/Regional Market district."[10] The number one goal that emerged from the FOCUS Greater Syracuse Vision Fair was to build leisure trails linking the suburbs and city for use by recreationalists and eventually commuters. In the past, a major stumbling block to the completion of the loop around the lake has been the cost of bridges that would cross Nine Mile Creek and Onondaga Creek Outlet. Recent legislation mandating the creation of plans for alternative modes of transportation, coupled with both private, state, and federal funds for the development of a continuous trail from Albany to Buffalo, give renewed hope that Onondaga Lake may finally achieve a trail to loop the lake. In 2002, the Haley Memorial West Shore Trail that stretches one-and-a-half miles is scheduled to be paved at the existing width of ten feet in order to retain its current natural appeal, as it journeys through what was once the heart of the Onondaga Lake resort district.

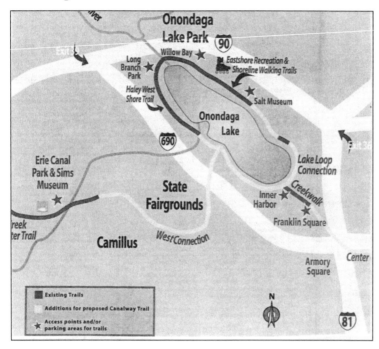

10.7 Portion of the Leisure Trails in Onondaga County Map, published by *Syracuse New Times*, 1999.

Signs of change in the old State Barge Canal terminal on the south shore of Onondaga Lake are beginning to bring to life a region in decay for decades. Contractors from the State Canal Corporation have repaired the harbor's concrete wall and have built "a pedestrian promenade" around the harbor, with trees and flowers lining the walkway. The Lakefront Development Corporation will be constructing 144 boat slips to transform the harbor into a marina. An amphitheater has been built for the west shore of the harbor where seating has been built into the hill facing the theater's stage. The picture that follows was taken in May 2000, from the Creek Walk Trail that runs along the west shore of the harbor, overlooking the repair work being done to the harbor's concrete wall.

Recently, the nearby Carousel Center announced that it will double its size over several years, giving additional financial initiative for the further development of the Inner Harbor to include retail shops and restaurants in an outdoor

10.8 Beginning stages of the Inner Harbor Revitalization, photo by author, May 2000.

setting to compliment the indoor mall businesses and attractions. The Lake Loop Creek Walk Trail would provide easy access from the mall via a bridge across Onondaga Creek to the Inner Harbor and to Franklin Square and beyond. The Inner Harbor amphitheater will bring outdoor performances back to the shores of Onondaga Lake, which have been missing since the golden age of the resort era one hundred years ago. At the moment a four-level aquarium featuring ocean life is planned for the mall and a fish and wildlife museum is planned for the Inner Harbor, all at a time when natural fish species are beginning to return to Onondaga Lake.

Several construction projects are going ahead to make Onondaga Lake a recreational asset to the region like it was one hundred years ago, but as witnessed by the past, rarely have these plans been fulfilled. The Army Corps of Engineers is working on plans to use new technology to clean up Onondaga Lake, but it has been hard to get local politicians to agree on a proposal before the court ordered cleanup deadline expires. One of the main polluters of the lake today remains the metropolitan sewage treatment plant, but plans to build a new plant on the south side of Syracuse to prevent raw sewage from overflowing into Onondaga Lake, have been met with fierce opposition from area residents. As the oil tanks have come down in Syracuse's Oil City neighborhood, plans to move ahead for the construction of Destiny USA, the expansion of Carousel Center Mall. This huge facility will cast a giant shadow on where the Iron Pier once stood. Politicians have struggled with a final tax plan for the Destiny USA project. It is hoped this project will have a positive impact on the use and enjoyment of Onondage Lake, much as the resorts and amusements did during the "Golden Age of Onondaga Lake Resorts"

In spite of many past obstacles, things look more hopeful, as planners and politicians seem to be working together better than in the past. Perhaps with state, federal, local, and private funding, and public interest and demand for additional recreational facilities, the hopes and dreams of the past century will come to fruition in the twenty-first century.

Afterword

During the years spent researching and interviewing to obtain material for this book, the author has developed a great appreciation for the rich heritage of Onondaga Lake. It is his hope that those who read this book will not only share this appreciation, but will support and even demand that our local and state officials will continue moving forward so that the long-discussed plans of restoration and development become a reality for future generations.

Notes

1. Robert W. Andrews, Second of a Five Part Series, "Onondaga Lake a Paradise Lost," *Syracuse Post Standard,* 15 October 1985.
2. Robert W. Andrews, Third of a Five Part Series, "Onondaga Lake a Paradise Lost," *Syracuse Post Standard,* 14 October 1985.
3. Robert W. Andrews, First of a Five Part Series, "Onondaga Lake a Paradise Lost," *Syracuse Post Standard,* 15 October 1985.
4. Onondaga Lake Review, A Publication of Atlantic States Legal Foundation, Inc. March 2000.
5. Robert W. Andrews, First of a Five Part Series, "Onondaga Lake a Paradise Lost," *Syracuse Post Standard,* 15 October 1985.
6. *Town of Geddes, 1776-1976,* prepared by the Geddes Bicentennial Committee, 1976.
7. Robert W. Andrews, Third of Five Part Series, "Onondaga Lake, a Paradise Lost" 16 October 1985.
8. Robert L. Voorhees, "Planners Envision Beautified Lake," *Syracuse Post Standard* 14 January 1951: p.1.
9. Sargent, Webster, Crenshaw and Folley, Architects, "West Shore Park on Onondaga Lake," Syracuse, NY, 1955.
10. "Down the Right Path", *Leisure Trails of Onondaga County, Syracuse New Times,* 2001.

Index

London Hippodrome, 40
Long, Dick, 83
Long Branch Entrances,
114-115
Long Branch Park, 21
Loomis, Nathaniel, 17
Loop the Lake, 133
Luna Park (Coney Island),
33
Lutheran Church of
Atonement, 117

Madison, William, 121
Mahzar, Fahreda, 74
Malaria, 127
Man-Made Desert, 66-67
Maple Bay Lakeside
Resort, 90-103
Mardi Gras of North, 55
Marl, 83
Markham, Charles, 88
Maroons, 26
Mason Judd (William), 81
Maurer, Ben, 105,
113-114, 116, 122
Maurer, Bernard, 121, 124
Maurer, Mrs. Bernard, 122
Maurer, George, 105
Maurer, Kermit, 112, 121,
123-124
Mauser Rifles, 99
McDonald, Arthur, 42
McGuire, James K., 43
McIver, F. F., 33-34
Melvin, Crandall, 65, 132
Melvin and Melvin Pony
Rides, 101
Mercury, 129-130
Metropolitan Sewage
Treatment Plant, 130
Meyers, Carl E., 57
Mikados, 26
Military Land Tract, 17
Miller, Rosey (John), 81
Milton, Tom, 44
Minting, Mr. (unicyclist),
40
Mitchell, Mason, 99
Mock Turtle Soup, 92
Mohawk Nation, 10, 13
Montcalm, Louis

Joseph de, 16
Murphy, Bret, 41
Mud Lock, 20, 39, 47,
65, 107, 131
Mud Lock Tavern,
126-127
Mulligan, George, 116
Mystique Krew, 40

National Protective
Legion, 117
Nichols Pond, 11
Nielezski, Lottie, 76
Nine Mile Creek, 60,
133-134
New York Central
Railway, 52, 57
New York State
Agricultural Society,
52, 55
New York State Fair, 33,
52
New York State Fair
Parking Lot, 67,
132-133
Newton, H.S., 94
Novelty, 99

Oil City, 135
Old Mill Ride, 38
Old Mill Chute, 113
Onondaga County
Emergency Work
Bureau, 14, 47, 65,
126, 131
Onondaga County Parks
System, 115
Onondaga County Park
And Regional
Planning Board, 133
Onondaga Creek, 16-17,
19, 23-24, 28, 30, 127,
129
Onondaga Lake –
Elevation, 8
Environmental Action
Plan, 133
Hiawatha Point, 10
Marina, 47-48
Outlet, 117
Parkway, 12, 14, 20,

132
Onondaga Nation, 123
Onondaga Yacht Club,
48-51
Oswego Canal, 18, 20, 39,
47, 65, 106, 108-109,
122, 126, 131
Oswego River, 8, 15
Otis Brass and String
Band, 63

Pain, the Fireworks King,
95-98
Parachute Jumps, 72
Peck, Fred R., 40
Pellegrini, Fred, 42
People's Railway
Company, 22, 24-26,
29, 106
Perry, Commander Oliver,
71
Petit, Eugene (steamboat),
108-109
Phelps, Professor, 93
Philadelphia Toboggan
Company, 111-113
Phippin, Frank, 121
Phoenix Dam, 75, 88
Phosphorus, 130
Pig Shoot Game, 123
Pinkowski, George, 65
Pitcher Hill of North
Syracuse, 120-121
Pleasant Beach Resort,
71-79
Powell Stock Farm, 53
Privies, 127
Prohibition Era, 77
Pugilists, 102
Pulaski Street, 15
Pyramid Construction
Company, 111

Radisson, Pierce, 14
Rasco, Sam J., 41
Rausch, John F., 26
Raut, Professor, 93
Rayon, 128
Reichert's Hotel, 75
Republican Club of
Geddes, 124